Storing Food Without Refrigeration

Carolyn Shearlock

Patoka Press
Indianapolis, Indiana

Storing Food Without Refrigeration, Third Edition
Copyright © 2024 by Carolyn Shearlock

Published by Patoka Press
An Adriane Doherty Company, LLC.
Indianapolis, Indiana
www.patokapress.com

Distributed by Cardinal Publishers Group
A Tom Doherty Company, Inc.
www.cardinalpub.com

ISBN: 978-0-99632-477-9
LCCN: 2018943657

Cover Design: Glen Edelstein
Cover Photos: Shutterstock
Editor: Dani McCormick, Tessa Schmitt
Book Design: Dave Reed
Interior and Cover Updates: Tessa Schmitt
Interior Photos courtesy of the author unless otherwise noted

Printed in the United States of America

10 9 8 7 6 5 4 3 2 1   18 19 20 21 22 23 24 25 26 27

The information provided within this book is for informational purposes only. Some of the information contained herein is directly contradictory to established US government recommendations for safe food storage. There is increased risk of illness or death due to storing food in some of the manners discussed herein. If you choose to follow the storage advice in this book, you assume all associated risks.

The author and publisher are not responsible for any illness that may come as a result of following the advice given in this book. Those with a weakened immune system or other underlying medical conditions should take extra precautions. There are no guarantees or warranties, express or implied, about the completeness, accuracy, reliability, suitability, or availability of the information, products, or services contained in this book for any purpose.

Contents

Dedication   ix

Preface   xi

Introduction   xiii

Buying Food   1
  General Food Buying Tips   2

Meat and Seafood   6
  Buying Canned Meat and Seafood   7
  Canning Your Own Meat   7
  Canned Meat and Seafood Meal Ideas   10
    Ham   10
    Chicken or Turkey   11
    Tuna and Salmon   11
    Crab   12
    Shrimp   12
    Corned Beef   12
    Roast Beef   13
    Clams   14
    Oysters   14
  Cooking with Canned Meats and Seafood   14
  Vacuum-Sealed Refrigerated/Frozen Meats and Seafood   15

Shelf-Stable Meats 18
Freeze-Dried Meats 20
Fresh Fish and Seafood 22

Produce 24
 Buying Fruits and Vegetables 25
 To Wash, or Not to Wash? 26
 Storage Basics 28
 Fruits and Veggies: Shortest to Longest-Lasting 30
 Storage Specifics for Various Vegetables and Fruits 35
 Stretch Your Stock of Fresh Fruit and Vegetables 50
 Canning Your Own Fruits and Vegetables 51
 Pickling Vegetables 51
 Kimchi 54
 Grow Your Own 54
 Dehydrated Vegetables 58
 Dried Fruit 62

Herbs & Spices 63

Milk 65
 Boxed Milk of All Types 66
 Cream 71

Butter or Margarine 76
 Storing Butter at Room Temperature 77
 Canned Butter 77
 Butter Bell 78
 Brining Butter 79
 Substitutes for Butter 81

Cheese 83

Powdered Cream, Sour Cream, Cheese and Butter 87

Eggs 89
 Unrefrigerated Eggs 90
 Powdered Eggs 92

Condiments   94
    Common Condiments   94
    The Clean Spoon Rule   95
    Horseradish and Wasabi   96
    Maple Syrup   96
    Mayonnaise and Miracle Whip   96
    Bottled Salad Dressings   97

Miscellaneous   99
    Coffee   99
    Canned Foods   99
    Juice   100
    Bouillon and Stock   100
    Tofu   101
    Leftovers   101

Cooler   103
    Setting Up a Cooler for Food   104
    What to Look For in Buying a Cooler for Food   107
    What Size Cooler to Store Food?   108

Putting It All Together   110
    Sample Four-Day Meal Plan   110

Final Thoughts   113
    Thank You So Much!   114

Appendix A: Instant-Read Thermometer Temps   115

Appendix B: Recipes   117
    Basic Vinaigrette   117
    Greek Dressing   119
    Olive Garden Copycat Dressing   121
    The Boat Galley Salad   123
    Three Bean Salad   126
    Healthier Zucchini, Carrot, or Sweet Potato Bread   128
    Yogurt   130
    Tasty Tuna Burgers   135

Tuna and Sweet Potato Patties 136
Chicken or Beef Enchiladas 137
Chicken or Shrimp Paella 138
Couscous Chicken 140
Chicken and Apricots 141
Roast Beef Chili 143
Pineapple Beef, Chicken, or Turkey 144
Goulash or Spanish Rice 146
Jambalaya 147
Pasta with Ham in Butter Sauce 149
Rice or Pasta Salad with Ham 150
Crab, Meat, Seafood, or Fish Cakes 151
New England Clam Chowder 154
Linguine and Clam Sauce 156
Ricotta Cheese 157
Chocolate-Oatmeal No Bake Cookies 159
John Herlig's Pickled Vegetables 161
Kimchi 163

Appendix C: Equivalent Measurement Chart 165

About Carolyn Shearlock 167

Index 169

Dedication

To everyone who has ever asked me a question about how to store food and create great meals without refrigeration, and particularly to those who asked me to put all the info together in one place.

To my husband Dave, who said "Sure!" to all my hare-brained travel ideas and who unwittingly became the crash test dummy as I explored various ways to store food without refrigeration.

To everyone else who has ever thought "Do I really need refrigeration?"

Special thanks to Pamela Douglas Webster, John Herlig, and Todd Morgan, who read an early draft and gave me valuable suggestions.

Preface

When I wrote *Storing Food without Refrigeration* in early 2017, I knew that people wanted to learn techniques to store food without refrigeration—those articles were some of the most-read on my website, The Boat Galley.

I never dreamed of the response I'd get: boaters, campers, and more wanted to learn everyday techniques for living without refrigeration—or for expanding their options if they had only a tiny refrigerator. They wanted to know about foods they could buy at local stores and ways to store them that made sense for everyday meals. They didn't want "hardship" meals, but a way of life that was sustainable for weeks or months.

The second edition was almost two-thirds longer than the first edition in response to questions and comments I received. In particular, more than fifty photos of products and storage solutions were added, more vegetables and products were discussed, a recipes section was created in the appendices, and many procedures were explained in greater detail.

Now, in the third edition, I've continued to add material based on reader questions and comments. Here, I've detailed storing another 25 more fruits and vegetables, added 17 more recipes, and generally added information throughout. It's another 30% longer than the second edition!

Enjoy your (great) meals!

Introduction

YIKES! No refrigeration? Seriously?!

Many of us have memories of some long-ago trip—camping, canoeing, backpacking, or boating—where we didn't have access to a refrigerator and maybe not even a cooler. We ate freeze-dried, just-add-boiling-water food in a bag. It provided sustenance but not much else.

Good news! You can make a wide variety of great meals without refrigeration. Food that tastes great, has texture, and has no blobs, and you don't have to rely totally on canned food either.

With the techniques in this book, you can have meat and seafood; fresh fruits and vegetables; milk and eggs; cheese, sour cream, and yogurt; and all the normal condiments without a refrigerator or cooler. If you do have a small refrigerator available—say in a boat or small RV—these techniques will help you make the most of the limited space by only using it for high-priority items.

You'll learn:

- Ways to store fresh food without refrigeration

- Great alternative products

- Which foods do not need to be refrigerated

- Ways to make sour cream, yogurt, and ricotta cheese from shelf-stable ingredients

- Techniques for cooking with canned meats to preserve flavor and texture
- How to set up a cooler to store food, if you're lucky enough to have one available

You'll also find more than 60 main dish ideas, and the final chapter provides a four-day sample meal plan.

Carolyn

Buying Food

"If I don't have refrigeration, where do I buy my food?"

Many people think that if they don't have refrigeration, they can't have fresh food. They can't have milk or eggs, and no fresh vegetables. They envision shopping almost exclusively in the canned foods aisle or in a specialty outdoors store.

You can buy all the food you need in a regular supermarket, in pretty much all of the aisles: produce; dairy; meat, either for the same day or longer if you have a cooler; and yes, some canned foods, too. If you have access to a farmer's market or produce stand, even better. Most of the things that I buy online or in specialty stores are either treats or backups to have on hand, not my core foods.

I asked a few friends who cruise without refrigeration to read an early draft of this book, and one of the comments I got back was that they didn't recall seeing many of the products I discuss in the grocery stores where they shopped. I'll admit, some take a bit of searching or asking at the customer service counter, but I've been able to buy almost everything I describe as "usually available in supermarkets" even at tiny grocery stores in towns with less than 2,000 people. Occasionally, however, even the large stores in a particular area won't carry an item. Shopping is part of the adventure!

In the sections that follow, I've tried to say what aisle I most often find things in if they're a little less common. I've also tried to give alternatives and good backups to keep on hand; some of these are more typically online purchases.

I also discuss brands of certain products that I like. No, I'm not being compensated by any of these companies. They are simply products that my husband and I like much better than other brands we've tried. Some taste better, some have longer shelf life, some have less sodium. I am certain that there are other good brands available; I know that I have not tried every brand of every item. So don't feel that you can't try other brands, but my suggestion with any new food—even the ones I like, as your tastes may be different—is to try one of an item before stocking up.

General Food Buying Tips

How long to plan and buy for?

When you are just starting to travel or live without refrigeration, it's easiest to create a meal plan and then build a shopping list from that. I suggest starting with maybe three days, then lengthening to a week once you get comfortable.

For trips longer than that, I don't bother with meal plans. Instead, I buy "for the pantry" and then decide each day what we'll have. This is particularly true on longer trips in remote areas where we may go up to a month between grocery stores.

To stock the pantry, I'll start by thinking about how often we use various foods and how much we eat at a time. So, if we basically alternate eggs and cereal for breakfast, and I'm stocking up for the next two weeks:

- Eggs = 2 each for my husband and I for 7 days = (2*2*7)

  = 28 just for breakfasts

- Cereal = 2 people for each of 7 days = 14 servings

- Boxed milk = the same 14 servings, in individual boxes for each day

2

Now, of course, if I think we'll have another dish that uses eggs, such as egg salad sandwiches for a lunch, or a quiche for dinner, I'll have to add that to the number needed. And the same for extra oatmeal if we want to make chocolate-oatmeal cookies.

When it comes to dinners, I may know that we tend to have ham twice a week, roast beef once, clams once, and so on. So for that two-week time period, I'd want 4 cans of ham, and two each of roast beef and clams. And right on down the line for everything else we typically eat – making one-week meal plans on your first trips gives you a good feel for how much you eat of each food item.

Other things, such as vegetable oil, I don't really think of in terms of "servings" but in terms of how long a container typically lasts and how much I already have on hand. Will I need more before I go shopping again? Will I nearly be out of the item? If so, it goes on the list.

Scan the QR code with your phone's camera app and click the link that appears!

If you'd like a spreadsheet to help you with food provisioning, I've created one that you can have for free. Be sure to read the included instruction sheet and modify it for the foods you want to have on your trip. Grab a copy and it will be emailed to you immediately.

Don't Expect to Change Your Preferences

Having no refrigeration doesn't mean that you have to make drastic changes in how you eat – and you shouldn't try to. For example, if you've never liked canned salmon, don't buy it just because it's there and your friend John says he loves it.

Believe me, you'll end up with those cans of salmon still sitting in the cupboard the next time you go to the grocery store. And the next, and the next. They're not going to suddenly look appealing. Same thing with other foods: if you don't like corn flakes, don't buy them just because they're on sale.

I like sauerkraut occasionally – maybe three or four times a year. So why did I buy a dozen cans when a friend told me they had a sauerkraut salad recipe? I don't know, but it was three years ago and I just finally used up the last can.

I know, it seemed convenient. But it went against everything I knew about what my husband and I ate. And so, these cans became an inconvenience: they took up space so I had less room for the foods we did like, and it seemed that I was constantly moving them out of the way to get to other items.

Bottom line: if you know you're unlikely to eat something, just don't buy it. It doesn't matter if it's a great deal, if it'd be convenient, if your best friend loves it (unless they'll be with you!), you're not going to eat it.

Try One First

When buying a new food or a new brand, always buy just one the first time and try it before stocking up. There can be surprising differences between brands, particularly regional brands. One may be much sweeter than you're used to, or a totally different texture.

Many times, the new item will be wonderful. But I've certainly found my share of things that just didn't appeal to us and I was very glad that I hadn't bought more than one.

Buying a case of something you're unsure of risks your food budget, storage space, and having food you enjoy eating. Don't be tempted!

Carrying Your Food Home

If you won't be using your own car to carry provisions from the store, consider four other options:

- Taxi, Uber, or Lyft

- Bike with baskets or a trailer
- Wagon – high sides and large wheels are best
- Backpack

Otherwise, you'll have to make multiple trips if you're doing more than buying food for just a couple of days.

Canned food doesn't take a lot of special care to transport – other than paying attention to weight, particularly if you have to carry it any distance. A typical can of vegetables will weigh right at a pound, and quart boxes of milk weigh two pounds, so the weight adds up quickly!

Eggs have to be protected from breaking. A single layer generally does best, in a container with a lid over it. Don't count on the carton alone to protect them sufficiently. I have a plastic box that is designed for a loaf of bread, and it works well for a carton of eggs, too. Just slide the carton in and keep it flat – it's tough enough that I can put it in the bottom of a backpack and then pile cans on top of it!

One trick that I've learned when I need more than a dozen or two eggs is to get flats of 30 eggs and stack them into a milk crate. They fit almost perfectly. You can put two or three of the flats into the bottom of the milk crate and then put bread or tortillas on top, as they're light enough not to break the eggs. This works both for getting them home from the store as well as storing long-term.

Produce has to be protected from bruising. It's critical. Getting produce home safely is a major part of having it last; bruised foods will start to decay immediately.

Tote bags are generally best for avoiding pressure points; put the hardiest vegetables and fruit in the bottom of the bags and the most delicate ones on top. Don't try to put too much into one bag! You'll have more usable food if you buy less and get it home without bruises.

If you're doing a big stock-up, be sure to allow enough time to get everything put away after bringing it home. But the good thing about provisioning day? All those special food treats that don't last but you can feast on today!

Meat and Seafood

Do you equate no refrigeration with no meat? Don't worry. There's no reason to give up meat if you don't want to. Canned meats are great in all sorts of recipes, not just as sandwich fillers, and will form the bulk of meat for meals without refrigeration. If you have a good cooler and ice, you can also have "fresh" meat for the first day or two in the form of commercially vacuum-sealed meats.

Look closely near the tuna cans in the grocery store and you'll find a wide variety of canned meats and seafoods.

Buying Canned Meat and Seafood

I primarily use the small cans of meat and seafood that are about the size of tuna cans, as well as some in pouches. The tuna-size cans and pouches are great for two people, although some foods only come in cans that are closer to the size of a soup can. I buy all of mine in regular supermarkets.

You can find the cans in most grocery stores in the same area as the cans of tuna. You sometimes have to look hard to find them, but I've always been able to find:

- ham (usually Hormel, not the large canned hams sold in the meat department, and not the small deviled hams)

- roast beef (typically Libby's)

- corned beef

- salmon

- crab

- clams

- chicken

You can also find oysters, anchovies, herring, corned beef hash, and more. Tuna and chicken are the only ones I consistently find in pouches as well as cans. Large national brands have always had good quality for me; other brands may be available locally, too.

If you have a larger group of people, Brinkman Farms (mail order with a few retail outlets) has very high-quality canned meats in 28-ounce (nearly 800 g) cans—enough to serve six people. With no refrigeration to store leftovers, they simply are not practical for one or two people.

Canning Your Own Meat

Canning your own meat is a good way to have larger pieces of meat, with firmer texture and less of a tendency to break apart. You'll also

7

Photo credit: Behan Gifford

Home canned meat is more flavorful and has better texture than store-bought if you have the equipment and are willing to spend the time.

PVC in a bin or storage locker adds an extra layer of protection for glass bottles and jars. While I use 4 inch (10 mm) PVC to accommodate wine bottles, 3 inch (7.5 mm) PVC is sufficient for most 4- and 8-ounce (125 and 250 ml) canning jars. Glue the PVC pieces together if not tightly wedged into a container.

know exactly what cuts of meat you're using and can use meats that are hard to find in commercial cans. Four-ounce (125 ml) jars work best for one person; eight-ounce (250 ml) jars for two. The one downside, of course, is having glass, although the risk of breakage can be lessened by putting jars in tube socks; I create special "jar storage" areas from PVC to lessen the chance of breakage still further.

Canning meat requires a pressure cooker large enough to hold the jars (you'll be a lot happier if you can process several at once) and, of course, the jars and lids. Lids can be tough to find in many foreign countries; if you think you might want to can outside the US, take a look at Tattler Reusable Canning Lids, available on Amazon. While not strictly necessary, a jar-lifter (tongs specifically designed for lifting jars out of boiling water) is a big help.

In short, canning meat requires sterilizing your jars and lids, cooking the meat, packing it into jars (you can also raw-pack it), adding liquid, putting the lids on, and then processing the jars under pressure. Once cool, put the jars into tube socks and pack securely in storage areas.

Canning your own meat takes equipment and a reasonable supply of water (and will make the kitchen hot and humid), but is totally do-able in home kitchens and most boat galleys. If canning on a boat, pick a calm anchorage to be working with so much boiling water! There are many online sources for directions, as well as many canning cookbooks. Pick a reputable, modern source as recommendations have changed considerably over the years. One of my favorites is the Oregon State University Extension Service, which has extensive information on canning just about anything. Of course, follow the directions carefully and never eat food that looks or smells suspicious.

Almost any recipe can be adapted to use canned meat. Use the list below to see the possibilities, then learn tips for creating great meals (not mushy blobs!) in the section following that.

Canned Meat and Seafood Meal Ideas

You can make a wide range of dishes using canned meat and seafood. Here are more than sixty meal ideas, and you'll discover that you can adapt many of your family favorite meals to use canned meat, too.

Ham

- Pasta Alfredo or pesto

- Ham cakes (basically crab cakes made with ham)

- Scrambled eggs with ham (good with onions, green peppers, cheese, tomatoes, too)

- Ham loaf

- Gumbo

Even without refrigeration, breakfast burritos are still an option—eggs, cheese, and veggies do not have to be refrigerated, as discussed in later chapters, and canned ham works wonderfully to add meat.

- Split pea soup and other bean soups

- Ham salad sandwiches

- Pasta primavera

- Jambalaya

- Hobo dinner (sautéed with potatoes, carrots and onions)

- Rice or pasta salad

- Breakfast burritos

- Potato soup

- Pizza

Of course, you can also buy a one- to five-pound (0.5 to 2.5 kilo) canned ham in the meat department and roast it with potatoes and carrots. Be sure not to get a larger one than you can eat if you don't have a way to keep leftovers chilled.

Chicken or Turkey

- Enchiladas

- Chicken paella

- Stir fry

- Hobo dinner (cooked in a foil packet with carrots and potatoes)

- Pesto pasta with mushrooms

- Soup

- Pasta primavera

- Chicken or turkey salad sandwiches

Tuna and Salmon

- Fish cakes (variation on crab cakes)

- Pasta Alfredo

- Rice or pasta salad

11

- Quiche (salmon is better than tuna)

- Salmon loaf (similar to meat loaf)

- Tuna casserole (use the same basic recipe with salmon and touch of dill)

- Tuna or salmon salad—make sandwiches or stuff a tomato

Crab

- Crab cakes

- Pasta Alfredo (particularly if you get lump meat)

- Stuffed tomatoes

- Crab Rangoon

- Crab dip

- Quiche

Shrimp

- Pasta Alfredo

- Shrimp cakes (like crab cakes but made with tiny shrimp)

- Stir fry—great with crunchy fresh veggies

- Pasta primavera

- Stuffed tomatoes

- Shrimp paella

- Rice or pasta salad

Corned Beef

- Meat cakes

- Sandwiches (best mashed up with some diced onion and ketchup)

Canned roast beef is the base for this sweet-and-sour dish, combined with a can of pineapple chunks and a few fresh veggies that store well without refrigeration.

Roast Beef

- Chili
- Goulash
- Spanish rice
- Enchiladas
- Spaghetti
- Hobo dinner (sautéed with carrots, potatoes, and onions)
- Stew or soup
- Beef stroganoff
- Paninis
- Meat pie

- Sandwiches—hot or cold
- Roast beef is also good just heated up!

Clams

- Clam chowder
- Linguine with clam sauce
- Paella

Oysters

- Jambalaya
- Oyster stuffing
- Paella
- Pasta with oysters
- Oyster stew

Don't forget things like herring, that are good for appetizers, and anchovies, that can be used with pasta or on pizza.

You can adapt your existing favorite recipes to use canned meat and seafood with the tips in the next section. Additionally, The Boat Galley Cookbook has over eighty canned meat and seafood recipes, neatly grouped to make them easy to find.

Cooking with Canned Meats and Seafood

It's not hard to prepare great meals from canned meats. The canning process tends to take away some of the firmness and flavor of the meat, so the trick is to preserve and enhance the texture and flavor that's there.

Many people have had bad experiences with meals from canned meats turning into one big blob of food rather than having identifiable ingredients. A few tips to keep this from happening:

- Don't try to brown canned meat. You won't get the same effect as with raw meat.

• Change the order that you add ingredients in the recipe. The canned meat is already cooked, so all you have to do is warm it up. Add it just before serving, then let the dish sit for three to five minutes for the meat to heat through.

• Once you've added the meat, stir the dish as little as possible, so it won't turn to mush. Chicken and turkey are especially susceptible to over handling; ham has the least problem.

• Crumble or break apart ham when you add it. All other meats should be handled very gently.

• Watch out for overcooking other ingredients to the point where they lose their texture and become a blob with the meat.

• Drain liquid from the can and use it in the cooking process instead of plain water (ditto for any canned vegetables you use). It'll add a lot more flavor!

• Canned meats work well in baked casseroles since they don't get stirred. Just don't try to brown the meat before using it in the casserole.

• Replace any salt in the recipe with bouillon powder or paste of an appropriate flavor to make up for the fact that you don't have drippings from browning the meat.

Vacuum-Sealed Refrigerated/Frozen Meats and Seafood

If you have a cooler or ice box, vacuum-sealed meats and seafood are available in almost every grocery store (be sure to read *Setting Up a Cooler for Food*). These are a great way to have fresh meat for the first day or two after provisioning, even longer if they start out frozen. Note that I'm talking about commercially vacuum-sealed meats and seafood. Meats that are home-sealed are not processed the same way and are not as safe to use in the less well-regulated temperatures of a cooler. As a side note, if you have a tiny refrigerator that you are trying to make the most of with this book, vacuum-sealed meats are a good choice as they can be stored longer without being frozen.

Vacuum-sealed meat comes in thick plastic with no air in the package. Look for heavily-sealed edges as in the photo.

So what is vacuum-sealed and what isn't? Just because something has an airtight plastic wrap does not mean that it is vacuum sealed. Vacuum-sealed packages have no air inside and heavily sealed edges. The plastic is also heavier than the "plastic wrap" that covers cut meat on Styrofoam trays. You'll find the packages in the refrigerated or freezer cases; some, such as fish fillets or chicken breasts, will have the individual vacuum-sealed pouches in a larger heavy-duty plastic bag, or sometimes on a Styrofoam tray with a layer of plastic wrap over them.

Bacon and hot dogs have long been sold in vacuum-sealed pouches, but in the past five years many others have become available: pork roasts, chicken breasts, steaks, smoked sausage and fish fillets are all available in my grocery store. I even recently found some expensive organic ground beef in vacuum-sealed packages. Many lunch meats are, too. Note: the plastic-wrapped tubes of ground beef and sausage are not vacuum-sealed.

To store vacuum-sealed meats and seafood, remove any overwrap, bags and Styrofoam trays from the pouches, but don't take the meat or seafood out of the vacuum-sealed pouch until you're ready to cook it. If you use block ice in your cooler, there's usually a gap between blocks or between the block and the side of the cooler where you can put the meat. With cube ice, you can push the pouches into or under the ice. Remember

Individually vacuum-sealed breasts should be taken out of their bag and frozen, then may be tucked into ice in a cooler.

that the coldest area of a cooler or ice box is at the bottom (heat rises, cold falls), so keep the meat as low as possible. Because vacuum-sealed packages are watertight, you don't have to worry if it sits in the cooler water.

The FDA states that unopened commercially vacuum-sealed pouches of meat and seafood can be kept unfrozen for up to two weeks if constantly kept below 40° F. (4° C.) If you have a good cooler and plenty of ice, you can tuck the vacuum-sealed pouches into the ice and they'll stay below 40° F. (4° C.) for several days (longer if they were frozen

17

when you put them in and/or you are able to replenish the ice).

While you could use a thermometer to make sure that the ice and melt water temperature stays below 40° F (4° C.). I've always used the rule set forth by Omaha Steaks (which ships vacuum-sealed meats with dry ice): as long as the package is cool to the touch, it is safe to eat.

Some local butchers will vacuum-seal and freeze meat for customers. As far as safety, they fall between commercially-vacuum-sealed meats and those that are home-sealed. If you have sufficient ice to keep them frozen, they can last quite a long time; once thawed, they should be eaten immediately.

Be sure to cook the meat to the FDA-recommended temperature to kill any bacteria that might be present (see Appendix A). If you're ever in doubt about meat being good, err on the side of caution and don't eat it!

Shelf-Stable Meats

A limited number of vacuum-sealed shelf-stable meats exist, too. Pepperoni is often sold in this way, as are a number of "smoked sausage" products. Shelf-stable pre-cooked bacon has become quite popular, and sometimes you can find ham, too. Jerky and Slim Jims also fall into this group. They do not have to be refrigerated until open, and most packages are sized so that you can use them up in a single meal.

Look for packages that are sold at room temperature in stores. Often similar products will be sold refrigerated and at room temperature, so be sure to get the ones that say "refrigerate after opening." Brands, products, and availability vary greatly, so it is difficult for me to make specific recommendations.

Pepperoni, ham, bacon, and hard sausages are good in:

- Pizza
- Pasta salads

Quiche—or mini-quiches—can be made with shelf-stable sausage or diced pepperoni. The Thrive freeze-dried sausage crumbles are also great used this way!

- Hot pasta dishes

- Loaded baked potatoes

- Omelets

- Soups

- Quiche

- Sandwiches

- Scrambled eggs

Let's not forget that pepperoni and hard sausage are great added to a plate of crackers, olives, and cheese for a happy hour treat or even lunch!

Freeze-Dried Meats

Freeze-dried meats have two distinct advantages over canned: they are lighter-weight, and the unused portion does not have to be kept cold. The disadvantage is that they are usually cut into small pieces and tend to disintegrate into powder as they are jostled in storage.

Freeze-dried meat can be added to a cooked dish (rehydrating as it cooks) or soaked for a couple minutes then added to a dish. The meat was good in tacos, but it was best when I had some fresh tomatoes to put on top instead of rehydrated tomatoes. Spanish rice and goulash were also good, as were gumbo and jambalaya. You cannot sauté or brown the meat.

I keep some freeze-dried meats (and veggies too) as a backup supply, but since they tend to produce that unidentifiable blob of food that I hate, I don't use them as my primary meat supply if there are other options. Freeze-dried meats are sometimes—but rarely—available in stores that

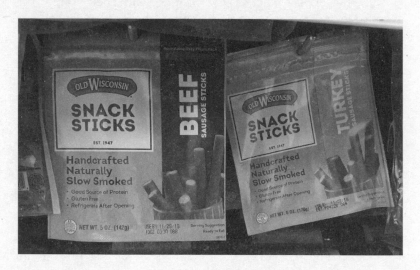

cater to backpackers, but generally have to be purchased online.

By far the best freeze-dried meat that I've found is the Thrive brand,

particularly their ground beef and sausage crumbles. They also have larger chicken slices than many other brands, but these have the same tendency to fall apart when stored in a moving vehicle or boat. Chicken, in general, is more fragile than beef or pork.

Unopened containers of freeze-dried meat should be stored where they won't be crushed or jostled too much – both will quickly turn the meat into dust. Once a container is open, it should be kept cool and dry. I usually put the contents of a bag or canister into a lockable gasketed lidded contained such as a Lock & Lock; it is essential to keep humidity out. Even just putting it inside a Ziploc bag is better than nothing. My experience is that the "resealable" pouches or cans just don't reseal tightly enough on their own.

The best way to rehydrate freezed-dried meat is to prepare the rest of the dish and then add the meat and about half of the recommended amount of water to the hot food. Stir very gently and briefly to mix the meat in. Put a lid on for 2 to 5 minutes and let sit. If the meat is not fully rehydrated then, heat for another 2 to 4 minutes but do not stir.

21

If you must rehydrate meat on its own, heat the recommended amount of water to boiling. I like to add some bouillon of an appropriate flavor and mix well. Then add the dried meat and stir just enough to get it down into the water. Put a lid on for 2 to 5 minutes and let sit. If the meat is not fully rehydrated then, heat for another 2 to 4 minutes but do not stir.

You should use freeze-dried meats in much the same way as canned meat, handling them as little as possible and very gently. You can also get "just-add-boiling-water" freeze-dried backpacking meals, but I recommend these only as a last resort. Using individual ingredients—even if they are all freeze-dried—and your own seasonings to make a dish almost always has better taste and texture.

Fresh Fish and Seafood

If you are near a body of water, fresh fish and seafood are always an option, whether you catch it yourself or buy it from a local fisherman. Depending on the circumstances, you may be able to keep live fish or seafood for a few hours in the water (fish on stringers, clams, shrimp, and lobster in net bags); once dead, the sooner it's eaten, the better. This is especially true if you can't keep it cold.

Ciguatera is the biggest risk with fresh saltwater fish. Most people only know a little about it and thus I want to discuss it a little even though it's really outside the scope of this book. It is a strange and potentially debilitating form of food-borne illness, unlike any other. Unfortunately, you can't tell if a particular fish carries ciguatera until you've eaten it and gotten sick.

Ciguatera is most often found in reef fish, and even there, amongst the top predators: barracuda and grouper. Recently, other fish have been found to carry it, even some pelagic fish. The best advice is to ask locals what fish to stay away from (it varies by area) but understand that there is always a risk.

If you do get ciguatera, you're generally not just a little sick, you're really sick with both gastrointestinal and neurological symptoms. Bad

news: there's no "cure" or antidote. Worse: symptoms can continue for months to years. Even worse: once you think you're cured, many things will trigger a new bout—alcohol (even a single beer or glass of wine for some people), nuts, and fish (even fish that doesn't make anyone else sick) are common triggers.

Symptoms of ciguatera poisoning can begin as little as fifteen minutes after eating a bad fish but are more likely to first appear six to twenty-four hours later. Gastrointestinal symptoms usually appear first—vomiting, diarrhea, intense stomach pain, and cramping—with neurological symptoms coming one to two days later. Symptoms can last from a few days to years.

The classic—and unnerving—symptom is that of temperature reversal. Hot items feel cold, and cold items hot. This can be seriously dangerous with people taking scalding hot showers or burning themselves on hot drinks. Luckily, not all people get this.

If you suspect you or anyone in your group has contracted ciguatera, seek immediate medical help.

Produce

Photo credit: Behan Gifford

Not sure how to store fresh fruit and vegetables without refrigeration? With a bit of care, many fruits and vegetables can be stored anywhere from one week to a month at room temperature. Others will last at least a few days without refrigeration and provide a post-provisioning treat. Canning, pickling, sprouting, and growing your own add even more options.

If you have a cooler or ice box to use for food, you can double the storage time for much of the more fragile produce.

Buying Fruits and Vegetables

For the longest life, buy never-refrigerated vegetables and fruit
at a true farmer's market where items are freshly picked.

Having produce last a reasonable amount of time without refrigeration
begins at the store or farmer's market. This is probably the most
important part of the process and the one usually overlooked. I've
learned my lesson the hard way—you simply can't go into the grocery
store, walk to the produce section, grab the first thing you see, and expect
to be able to keep it for any length of time without refrigeration.

Four things to keep in mind:

• Buy never-refrigerated fruits and vegetables if you can. These
are most often available at farmer's markets or produce trucks.
Once something has been refrigerated, condensation will form on it
when taken out of the refrigerator. Unless you are careful to dry it
completely, it will quickly get some bad spots, leading to rot.

• Be very picky. Pick over individual items and don't accept any that are bruised, rotten, overripe, have insect holes or look "old." Only the freshest, most perfect fruits and veggies will do. If you have to choose between perfect-but-refrigerated items and less-perfect, never-refrigerated items, go for the perfect.

• Don't buy too much. If you buy more than can comfortably fit in your storage areas, your fruits and vegetables will get bruised as you try to cram the extras in. Be realistic about how much room you have.

• Transport the produce gently. If you're carrying them in a backpack, bring along some towels to pad your purchases and don't cram them in. If you're going by car, make sure nothing will fall on them and they won't roll around. You don't want them bruised before you get home!

To Wash, or Not to Wash?

We get really spoiled with the produce we buy in US supermarkets: almost all of it has been washed long before we buy it. Much of it is even labeled "pre-washed—ready to use." But if you're outside the US—or buy your fruits and vegetables at a farmer's market or roadside stand— the question comes up of whether you should wash it immediately or just before using.

The argument for washing is to get any bugs off before they cause damage or infest other food, and also to have food ready to use when you want it. The argument against washing is that produce lasts longest with the least handling and left in the dirt it was pulled from. There's logic on both sides.

The reality is that, even at farmer's markets, I've rarely found produce that hasn't been washed at least once, so it's not in its own dirt.

In washing the produce, you're doing three things: getting any remaining dirt off, removing bugs, and getting rid of any germs and bacteria. I recommend it.

To wash, use one capful of bleach (plain, no fancy scent) in one to two gallons of water and swish your produce around in it. Depending on how much produce you have, you might even get by using a smaller container of the bleach solution (use a half-cap of bleach in a half gallon of water, etc.)—the important thing is to use enough to swish your items around and get any bugs off, not just give them a quick dunk. For tough, dirty items like carrots, use a vegetable brush to scrub the dirt off.

Berries are the one thing that take a bit of a different approach: instead of using a bleach solution, use a 1:10 vinegar to water solution. Swish the berries around and carefully pick out any that are getting soft.

Thoroughly drying your product is absolutely critical. If it's warm out, you may just be able to lay the produce on some towels for a half hour or so to dry it. Turn items over periodically so that there are no damp spots. On cooler days, it can pay to aim a fan at the produce to improve air flow. You can change towels periodically and even blot the water off.

The important thing is that you have to get the fruits and vegetables totally dry before storing them. Even in ventilated bins or gear hammocks, produce won't totally dry if put in damp—it will just start to rot.

As you put things away, double check each item to make sure it's in good condition. I usually find an item or two that need to be eaten right

Lay produce out to dry thoroughly before putting in storage bins.

away, which can be worked into the dinner menu.

Storage Basics

Storage areas need to be well-ventilated, dry, and as dark as possible. Bins need to be easily washable—plastic works the best as you can use bleach on it and it dries quickly. My choice is bins with solid bottoms and ventilated sides. Solid bottoms are good as they will contain the mess should one item rot. Do not use plastic lids on bins—light towels or rags laid over foods provide much better ventilation and allow you to put more in the bins.

Wire baskets and gear hammocks cause pressure points that will bruise, so these need to be well padded. That said, gear hammocks are generally good for storing veggies if they can be hung in locations where they won't bump into anything as the boat or vehicle moves, but will just

Bins with solid bottoms ensure that if any food rots, it will be easy to clean up. Much as I don't like plastic in general, it's easy to wash and sanitize with bleach. Ventilation holes on the sides allow air to flow, making spoilage less likely.

swing unencumbered.

Additionally, the bins and other storage containers need to be located where you can see into them to check on the produce daily. If you see something that's bruised, put it on the dinner menu. Anything that you missed and is now rotting or molding needs to be thrown out immediately—and the container wiped out with bleach. A quick tip: if you see fruit flies, check your produce extra carefully as bugs are

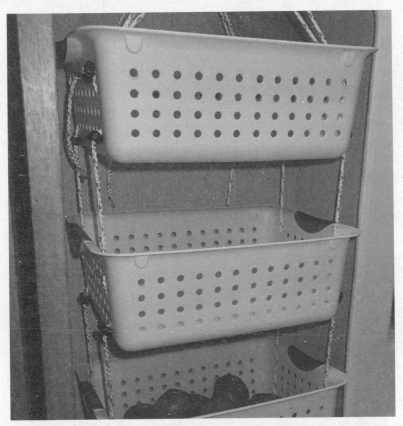

I repurposed a hanging locker in our boat to hold three large Sterilite bins for storing fruit and veggies. The air circulation is good around and through the bins. I use bungee cords to keep them from swinging excessively underway. A similar system can be created in RVs or even in the back of a vehicle for tent camping expeditions.

particularly attracted to produce that's bruised or spoiling.

I never store non-refrigerated produce in plastic bags—the bags simply trap any moisture and the food rots. I've tried the "green bags" and had the same results.

Hanging bins can be used to make storage space in otherwise unused areas—the shower, out-of-the-way corners and even a hanging locker if you don't have many hanging clothes.

Fruits and Veggies: Shortest- to Longest-Lasting

Almost all fruits and veggies will last a day without refrigeration, so provisioning day (or the first day of a trip from home) has a wide variety of choices. As days go on, use progressively longer-lived items. Potatoes, onions, cabbage, hard squashes and citrus fruits all last a surprisingly

A little attention to storage specifics and you can have sweet peppers, carrots, tomatoes and green onions for weeks, in addition to the more common potatoes and onions.

long time without refrigeration. Luckily, they can be used in a variety of recipes so that meals don't get boring even after a month. We also mix canned, dried, dehydrated, and fresh items so that there is almost always some fresh component in every dish.

The table below shows the average time that various fresh fruits and vegetables will last without refrigeration, when purchased unblemished and stored according to the instructions in the next section. Cool temperatures will prolong the storage time; tropical heat, high humidity, or enclosed vehicles will decrease it.

Fruits and Vegetables	_How Long Lasting_
Green Beans	Same day or pickle
Snow Peas	Same day only
Spinach	Same day only
Corn	Same day only
Chard and Kale	1 day, best same day as purchased
Berries (blueberries, raspberries, blackberries, strawberries)	1 to 2 days
Peaches and Apricots	Unripe peaches and apricots will take 1-3 days to ripen, then they will last 1-2 days
Lettuce and other Greens (leaves; heads that cannot be placed in water)	2 days at most, best same day as purchased
Bananas	2 days
Bok Choy	2 days
Artichokes	2 days
Tomatillo	2 days
Peas	2-3 days
Okra	2-3 days
Plums and Kiwi	Unripe, will take 2-3 days to ripen; Ripe, will last another 2-3 days
Grapes	2-4 days
Cherries	3 days
Kohlrabi	3 days
Lettuce and Greens (heads in water)	3-4 days

Asparagus	3-4 days
Eggplant (whole)	4 days
Brussels Sprouts	4 days
Broccoli	Few days to one week
Cauliflower	Few days to one week
Mushrooms	Few days to one week
Rhubarb	3-7 days
Pears	Unripe pears will take up to one week to fully ripen; Ripe pears will last 2-4 days (2 days in a hot climate)
Cucumber	Up to one week uncut; 1-2 days cut
Avocados	Up to one week
Napa Cabbage	One week
Cantaloupe and Honeydew	Unripe will take up to one week to ripen, then will last another week if uncut. Once cut, it will last 1-2 days
Rutabega	One week
Watermelon	One week (uncut)
Beets, Turnips, and Parsnips	One week, possibly longer
Summer Squash and Zucchini	One week to ten days (uncut)
Carrots and Celery	One to two weeks
Pomegranates, whole	One to two weeks
Mangoes	Ten days to two weeks
Peppers - sweet and hot	Ten days to three weeks
Pineapple	Two weeks

Tomatoes	Fully green tomatoes will take about two weeks to ripen; Once ripe, eat within two days
Citrus (oranges, grapefruit, lemons, limes)	Two weeks to one month
Radishes	Two weeks to one month, or more
Cabbage (head) - red or green	One month
Apples	One month
Acorn, Spaghetti, and other hard squashes	One month
Green Onions, Scallions, and Leeks	One month or more, depending on how often green tops are cut
Potatoes - white or sweet	2-3 months in cool climates; One month in tropics
Onions - white, yellow, or red	2-3 months in cool climates; One month in tropics
Jicama	6 months if temperature is under 60° F. Progressively shorter if warmer; One month in tropics

My veggie bin after a shopping trip, with Napa cabbage,
baby potatoes, mini peppers, carrots, whole mushrooms and
tomatoes. The green tomatoes are ripening in a tube sock
under the red ones.

Storage Specifics for Various Vegetables and Fruits

Onions

Store yellow, white, and red onions in a dark, dry area to keep them
from sprouting. One popular way to store them is to put onions in
pantyhose with a knot between each one. You can hang the resulting
strings of onions but make sure they won't bang into a hard surface
underway. Just cut them apart to use. You can also store onions in plastic
bins with a cloth over the top—do not use plastic over the top as they
need to be ventilated. Do not store onions and potatoes together as the
potatoes will sprout.

Green onions are among the easiest vegetables to store
and as a bonus, the tops will regrow several times!

Green onions, scallions, and leeks

Store green onions, scallions, and leeks as if they were cut flowers in a glass of water. Change the water every few days and don't be surprised if they continue to grow. If your water contains enough chlorine that you can smell it, let the glass of water sit for several hours to let the chlorine dissipate before adding the green onions, scallions, or leeks. If you use only the green tops, stick the white bottoms with roots back in the water. The tops will grow back several times!

Potatoes

Both white and sweet potatoes are some of the longest-lasting veggies if you take just a bit of care in storing them. For the longest life—two to three months in cool climates; generally a month in the tropics—store potatoes in a bin in a location that is:

- Cool

- Dry
- Dark (otherwise they'll turn green; you can simply put a towel over them, don't use a plastic bag)
- Away from onions (they'll sprout faster if near onions)
- Not in plastic bags (condensation will form in the bag and they'll rot)
- No pressure points (as occur with wire baskets; they'll bruise and then rot)

If potatoes turn greenish, peel them before use so that there is no green showing. If they sprout or have a bad spot, just cut the undesired area out when using. If potatoes are slightly soft or spongy without having rotten sections, they are simply dried out and will rehydrate as they cook.

Cabbage

Keep cabbage cool. Wrapping it in newspaper or an old t-shirt will help protect it from bruising, but I've had it last a month even without. Discard outer leaves before using if they pick up newspaper ink, get bruised or dry out. If the cut edge of the head develops some black spots, simply cut a thin slice off and discard—the rest of the head will still be good. Lettuce does not keep well without refrigeration, so cabbage becomes the salad staple.

Napa cabbage is a compromise between regular cabbage and lettuce—it is hardier than lettuce, but a little softer than regular cabbage—great for salads. It will last a week wrapped in a damp cloth and placed in a cool, ventilated place. Do not put any type of cabbage in plastic bags.

Brussels Sprouts

Store brussels sprouts the same way as cabbage but they'll only last about 4 days. Remove yellow outer leaves before cooking.

Rhubarb

Remove the leaves, leaving the stalks only (the leaves are toxic to people and animals). Place in a dry location. Whole stalks will last 3 to 7 days, depending on the temperature. Do not chop stalks until ready to use.

Carrots and Celery

Both will last a few days with no special treatment. For longer storage, I wrap both in aluminum foil but don't totally seal the packet, leave little openings at the ends for moisture to escape (otherwise, they'll just rot). A friend says she has good luck wrapping hers in slightly damp tea towels. Both carrots and celery may dry out some and look wilted but are easy to rejuvenate by soaking in water when you're ready to use them (if you will be cooking them in liquid, there's no need to rejuvenate first). They'll easily last one week, often 2 weeks or more.

Putting wilted celery or carrots in a glass of water for a half hour or so will restore the crispness and crunch. Despite what you may have been taught, the water does not have to be cold.

Artichokes

Artichokes don't last long without refrigeration but you can keep them for a couple of days. Don't wash. Trim a bit off the bottom and put in a shallow dish with ¼" unchlorinated water. Add water daily as needed. Do not put in a plastic bag or cover with plastic.

Cucumbers

Cucumbers, uncut, will last up to a week at temperatures between 40^0 F and 68^0 F if wrapped tightly with plastic wrap and protected from bruising. As the temperature rises, they'll last a progressively shorter time, even when wrapped. Once cut, they'll last a day or two at most.

Green, red, yellow, and orange peppers

Pad these well so they don't bruise and they will last at least one week. Once cut, they don't last long, so plan to use any leftover portion within a day and cut the edges off before using again. Both last much better if they can be put in a cooler, particularly after they've been cut.

A good alternative to "regular" peppers is bags of mini sweet peppers as you can usually use a whole one at a time. They will last anywhere from ten days to three weeks if kept cool and protected from bruising. They may look a little wilted after ten days, but the flavor is still good, and while they can still be used raw, they are then best in cooked dishes where it's not apparent. Leave them in the bags they come in—they have holes to let condensation escape. Pad them well so that they don't bruise.

Hot peppers

Store in the same manner as green peppers. Smaller peppers, such as cayenne, will slowly dry if in in well-ventilated container. I've used them up to a year later. They cannot be reconstituted, but work well as a spice.

Asparagus

Cut ½" (1 cm) off the bottom and stand upright in a glass with an inch or two (2 to 5 cm) of water, then place a plastic bag over the top to keep asparagus tips from drying out. These are best if in shade as less

Mini peppers are great for storing without refrigeration,
as you can use an entire one at a time. I bought these loose
at a farmer's market and just stored them in a bowl.

Store asparagus in a glass with a bit of water and a bag
over the top to keep the tips from drying out.
A wonderful treat a couple days after provisioning!

condensation will form in the bag. They will easily last three to four days; sometimes longer if it's cool.

Summer squash and zucchini

Small ones last much better than larger ones; they will last ten days or sometimes longer. If they are starting to wilt a bit, use them in a cooked dish instead of eating raw—you won't notice that they're not crisp.

Eggplant

Despite looking oh-so-similar to summer squash and zucchini, eggplant will only last about 4 days without refrigeration. Leave them whole and store in a dry, ventilated location. Absolutely do not store in a bag.

Spaghetti squash, acorn squash, and other hard squashes

These will last a month without refrigeration if protected from bruising, although once they are cut, the entire squash must be used—that is, you can't use half a squash one day and plan to use the rest next week. No other special treatment is needed. While they take up more space than some other veggies, they are great choices if you still want something fresh towards the end of longer trips.

Broccoli and cauliflower

These can both last a week, providing they've never been refrigerated. Both spoil very quickly—in just a day or two—if they've ever been refrigerated. Broccoli may get a little yellow, and cauliflower may get some black spots—just cut the discolored parts off. If either is a little less than perfect, use it in a cooked dish, and it won't be noticeable.

Lettuce

My experience with lettuce is that it is extremely susceptible to bruising, even if you can keep it chilled in a cooler. Bruised leaves then quickly rot. Eat it within a day—at the most two—of purchase. Whole romaine leaves or complete heads sold in plastic boxes have a longer life than other types of greens or other packaging.

Whole heads of greens

Another good technique for whole heads of various greens is to put them in a bucket of water with the stem down. A clean five-gallon (twenty-liter) bucket works best, with a few inches (5 to 10 cm) of water in the bottom, then stand the lettuce and other heads of greens upright and toss a light cloth over the top to keep the greens shaded and bugs and birds out. Celery, asparagus, green onions, and herbs can also be stored standing up in the same bucket.

If the bucket is not full enough to prevent bruising, add clean rags, or recycle Styrofoam chunks or bubble wrap to take up space while being gentle on the greens. Change water every day or two. If not bruised when purchased or in transport, I've had greens last four to five days stored this way.

Best candidates are heads of romaine, beet greens, and other greens sold in heads or clumps. Iceberg lettuce does not do well, nor do cut or picked greens such as most kale, spinach, or arugula. Friends report that dandelion greens do very well!

Bok Choy

Store bok choy like flowers – cut a sliver off the bottom and then place in a glass or bucket of unchlorinated water. Add water as needed. Fine to mix with other veggies (such as green onions, whole heads of greens, chard, and kale) that are also stored in a glass or bucket of water.

Chard and kale

Also store chard and kale like flowers, although they will only last about one day. If the chard or kale have been chopped, must be eaten the same day as purchased.

Mushrooms

Mushrooms either store well or horribly, often for no apparent reason. Do not wash until you are ready to use them. If you are putting them in a cooler, leave them in the package they came in with the plastic wrap over the top (it's designed with the optimum air holes to keep them moist but not rotting). They will generally last in very good condition for two to four days. If they dry out, they're still fine to use in cooking. If they get slimy, discard them.

To store without a cooler, remove them from the store packaging and place into a flat container where they are no more than two deep. Put it in a very well-ventilated location and do not cover. The mushrooms will dry out day by day (how quickly depends on the exact conditions) but can stay edible for a month or more in the right conditions. Turning them over every day or two will prolong their life so that they dry evenly. Use them in cooking and don't try to re-hydrate to eat raw.

Tomatoes

Buy tomatoes in varying stages of ripeness, from green to fully ripe depending on when you want to use them. Fully green tomatoes will last about two weeks as they slowly ripen; partially ripe ones less. Store the not-yet-ready-to-eat ones in a dark place, wrap with paper towels or newspaper, or keep them in tube socks—they need darkness to ripen. Check them daily and unwrap when ripe. Once ripe, tomatoes should be eaten within two days.

Tomatillos

Tomatillos will last 2 days, occasionally longer, if you put them in an open basket with the husks still on. Make sure that the basket is ventilated and in a location where air can move around it.

Okra

Okra will last 2 to 3 days. Store loose in a dry, ventilated location. Do not leave them in a bag.

Peas

Unshelled peas will last 2 to 3 days. Store loose in a dry, ventilated location and shell immediately before using.

Store green tomatoes in a tube sock. Put the greenest one in first, then progressively less green ones to make it easy to check on them and remove them when ripe. Once fully red, eat within two days.

Radishes

Cut green tops off, leaving only about ½" (1 cm) of the leaf stem. Basically, you don't want to cut the top of the radish itself. You can wash the radishes now or when you use them. Store wrapped in a slightly damp cloth (old towel or t-shirt works well) or place in a container of slightly damp sand (it's okay if the sand is dampened with salt water). Every few days, remove the rag, rinse it, wring it out, and re-wrap the radishes.

If using sand, make sure that the radishes are completely covered and the sand is only damp, not wet. Theoretically, using sand should give you longer storage times, but I have found that it's easier to get the "slightly damp" condition with a cloth. Radishes will last anywhere from two weeks to more than one month (in cool locations, storage up to several months is possible), making them great for a burst of flavor and crunch long after many other choices are gone.

Produce

Beets

Cut the greens off the top of the beet, leaving at least one inch of stem to avoid the beet "bleeding." Use greens within a day. Knock any excess dirt off but don't wash or scrub until you're ready to use the veggie. Put beets in a bowl and cover with a damp cloth; be sure cloth stays damp. Beets will last a week, longer in cool temperatures.

Beets can also be buried in a five-gallon bucket of damp sand, sawdust or peat moss, but can't be allowed to touch one another (they'll rot where they touch) so don't pack them too tightly! Do not seal the container. Beets can last a month or more packed this way if temperatures are cool—in tropical temperatures, they'll typically last only a week or two.

Turnips and parsnips

Store in same manner as beets, above, but there is no need to leave the stem on. Similarly they can be stored in sand, sawdust, or peat moss – and can't touch one another.

Kohlrabi

Kohlrabi likes cool temperatures and does best under 40^0 F. It needs nothing special, other than to be protected from bruising, for up to 3 days. After that, it's best to pack them in dry sand, as for beets above but the sand must be dry. Again, don't let them touch one another. Even in sand, they'll only last a week or maybe less in tropical temperatures; longer as the weather gets progressively cooler.

Rutabega

Rutabega also likes cool temperatures – the closer to freezing the better. Store unwashed, wrapped in a moist towel, for up to 7 days. Figure that it will last one day less for every 7 degrees that the average temperature is over 35^0 F. Don't try to store rutabega if the temperature will be over 80^0 F, but just eat the same day as purchased.

Jicama

Jicama might win the award for longest-lasting veggie with no refrigeration. Just keep it in a cool, dry location, preferably with no citrus nearby. If temperatures are less than 60^0 F, it can last three months. Storage time gets progressively less as the average temperature gets warmer, to about one month in tropical climates. Once cut, jicama must be eaten within two days or the leftovers refrigerated.

Citrus fruits

Wrap citrus fruit individually in aluminum foil and do not store near apples (will cause the apples to rot). It's very important to make sure that items are completely dry before wrapping in foil. In foil, they will last several weeks to one month, even longer in cool climates. Unwrapped, fruits will last one week to ten days on average. Minor mold on the skin can be wiped off with a mild bleach solution.

Bananas

We have never been able to keep bananas longer than two days—they bruise much too easily. If you can find green bananas (we never could), they will last about a week—but they'll all ripen at once.

Buying a stalk of 100 or so green bananas and tying a bag around it to allow just one round to be exposed—and ripen—at a time sounds like a wonderful idea for an ocean passage. However, the boaters that I've known to try this have ended up with the entire stalk (not just one round) all ripening at once. I have heard their horror stories of the bugs that crawled out of the stalk. I'd call it a great idea that fails in practice.

Mangoes

Buy mangoes in varying stages of ripeness from ripe (to eat right now) to rock hard (to eat in ten days to two weeks). As the rock-hard ones ripen, they'll ooze a bit of juice, so store them in their own bin with clean rags that can be easily washed. Check daily and replace the rags as needed so as not to attract ants and other bugs.

Peaches and apricots

Unripe peaches and apricots are rock hard; ripe ones will give a little in your hand but won't feel soft. Unripe peaches and apricots will only take 1 to 3 days to ripen; less time if they are stored near other ripening fruits. Once ripe, eat within a day if in a hot climate or two days if in cooler temperatures.

Avoid bruising your peaches and apricots! Use soft rags to pad them; do not use plastic or bubble wrap as both promote rot. Lay both peaches and apricots in a single layer as the weight of another piece of fruit on top can cause bruising.

If peaches get a little too soft but are not moldy, use them in a cooked dish such as peach cobbler; you can use the same basic recipe to make apricot cobbler, which is delicious with overripe apricots.

Plums and kiwi

Like peaches, test for ripeness by gently squeezing the fruit. Ripe ones will give slightly but not be soft. Buy ripe ones to eat in the next 2 – 3 days; unripe ones to eat another 2 – 3 days beyond that. Similarly, if plums get a little softer than you'd like, use them in a cooked dish – one of my favorites is to dice them and make plum muffins. I've never discovered anything that was great with kiwis that were getting soft.

Plums are a little hardier than peaches, and kiwis a little hardier yet. They still both need to be protected from bruising and shouldn't be wrapped in plastic. Plums can be stored two deep; kiwis, three deep.

Pears

Test pears for ripeness by pressing on the neck with your thumb. If fully ripe, they will give a little (if they give a lot, they're overripe). If they're rock hard, they're unripe – but there is no change in color as they ripen, so it's almost impossible to tell how close to ripe they are. This makes it hard to buy a "continuing supply" that will ripen in sequence. You just have to check them every day and eat within four days of becoming ripe (if in a hot climate, they'll probably last only two days).

If you want to speed up the ripening, place near bananas or apples. They will also ripen faster near unwrapped citrus, but not wrapping your citrus will cause it to have a much shorter life.

Use soft rags to pad the pears in almost any type of container, but do not cover them. Bruising is the biggest problem with pears, either from rough handling, bouncing around, or pressure spots. Small bruises (brown spots) can be cut out when eating. To help prevent bruising, store pears in a single layer.

Apples

Apples will last up to one month if you can protect them from bruising. Don't store with citrus (will cause the apples to over-ripen) or bananas (will cause the bananas to over-ripen). Tarter varieties store better than sweet ones. "Delicious" apples, in particular, tend to degrade in texture, if not taste. If apples are not chilled, they won't have as much crunch.

Pineapple

Pineapple will last up to two weeks if purchased green, but don't eat them until they are fully ripe. Pad them well against bruising and keep them upright. Once ripe, cut the entire pineapple up—any slices not eaten immediately should be eaten within a day if not in a cooler. The pieces will last two to three days in a cooler.

Berries (strawberries, blueberries, raspberries, etc.)

Berries will only last two days at most without a cooler and are better the first day. My suggestion: buy and eat the same day! In a cooler, they can last three days if rinsed with vinegar, protected from bruising, and if any bruised berries are removed immediately.

Berries that start to go soft, but aren't moldy, are good in cobblers and muffins.

Cherries

Store cherries in same manner as berries (including rinsing with vinegar), but they will typically last three days at room temperature; about one week in a cooler.

Grapes

To store grapes, remove them from plastic bags and place in bins on clean rags—they may ooze some juice. Check them daily and change rags as needed so as not to attract ants. They will usually last at least two, often as many as four, days. After that, they may start to dry out, but still won't mold for several more days—sometimes never. They are edible as long as they don't rot or mold. The older, drier ones are great used in coleslaw or tuna salad!

Avocados

Avocados are fairly susceptible to bruising and require careful handling to have them last beyond a day. The best way I've found to store them is to put them in tube socks, then in a gear hammock or bin on top of a towel or other padding over "sturdy" produce such as potatoes or onions. If you buy them in varying stages of ripeness—with some still rock-hard—you can enjoy them over a week or more. Once fully ripe, avocados need to be eaten within a day. Expect at least one in four to bruise so badly as to be inedible. Don't try to save a part of an avocado; use an entire one at a time.

49

Papaya

Store papayas the same as avocados. Unripe papaya are green and rock hard. Fully ripe, they are yellow-orange with very little green color and give a little when gently squeezed. Rock hard, they'll take about a week to fully ripen; once ripe they should be eaten within two days. Again, like avocados, don't try to save part of one.

Watermelon

Watermelon is great if you're having a get-together in a few days with a bunch of people. It will last a week if left whole and is relatively hard to bruise. Just put it somewhere that it won't roll or fall. Once cut, it should be eaten the same day or small pieces can be kept in a cooler for 3 to 4 days (cut the rind off so that they don't take up so much space).

Cantaloupe and honeydew

Cantaloupe and honeydew will nicely ripen on the counter in about a week. Both are generally shipped unripe as they bruise far less that way, so unless you buy your melon from a farmer, assume that it's unripe. When ripe, both will have a little give when pressed on the end opposite the stem – but won't be soft. Once ripe, they'll last uncut on the counter for up to one week (less in a hot climate); once cut, eat within a day or at the most, two.

Put an airy, soft rag over the cut melon to keep flies off.

Pomegranates

Pomegranates are generally shipped ripe. Whole, they'll last one to two weeks if protected from bruising and direct sunlight. Seeds must be kept in a cooler if not eaten within a few hours.

Stretch Your Stock of Fresh Fruit and Vegetables

Make your stock of fresh veggies last longer by combining fresh, canned, and dried ingredients into a single dish. Salads are a great way to do this, such as:

- Chopped cabbage with dried dates or raisins and either a vinegar or mayonnaise dressing for coleslaw

- Canned green beans with fresh tomatoes and onions and a vinaigrette dressing

- Diced boiled potatoes, chopped onions, and canned green beans make a great potato salad

- Shredded cabbage with a can of mandarin oranges or pineapple and a handful of peanuts, mixed with mayonnaise or Miracle Whip for a not-your-everyday coleslaw

Canned green beans, in particular, make a great substitute for lettuce in salads. You can make your own vinaigrette dressing; see page 117 for storing mayonnaise and other condiments without refrigeration.

Other fresh and canned options include oven- or skillet-roasted vegetables using combinations of fresh and canned: sweet potato chunks, onions, canned green beans, and canned or fresh mushrooms is one of our favorites. Even just adding fresh onions to a dish (instead of dried or onion powder) makes a big difference.

Canning Your Own Fruits and Vegetables

If you have access to a farmer's market, canning your own fruits and vegetables can produce tastier and better textured results than commercially-canned. As with canning your own meats (page 7), it takes some bulky equipment, time, and a willingness to have glass aboard. A water bath or—better yet—pressure processing is highly recommended to prevent any chance of food poisoning. Food poisoning is bad anywhere, but if you are days from medical help, it's even worse.

Pickling Vegetables

Pickling vegetables can take three different forms: traditional pickling for long-term storage, quick pickling and, as no-refrigeration cruiser John Herlig recently explained to me, pickling just to create a new taste. And don't just think of pickling cucumbers—carrots, onions, broccoli,

51

cauliflower, corn, asparagus, beans, beets, okra, sweet or hot peppers, and mushrooms are all good candidates. Cabbage—in the form of sauerkraut—is also great.

Traditional pickling can be done by fermentation—putting the vegetables in a large crock with a very precise mixture of vinegar, salt and water—and letting it sit for a month or more until the vegetables ferment, then canning or refrigerating them to stop the fermentation.

It can be a problem to keep a container out for that long. If temperatures get over 80^0 F (26^0 C) the pickles will get soft. In years past, these were the type of pickles that you'd see out in a crock or barrel, kept at room temperature until they were all eaten, with the scum skimmed off every day.

Canned green beans, dried dates, black beans, quick-cooking couscous, fresh tomatoes, and onions make a great salad. Top with a simple make-your-own vinaigrette that doesn't need refrigeration.

Quick pickles are a better option for most of us. Basically, vegetables are packed into sterile jars (with any herbs or spices desired) and a hot vinegar solution poured over the top. Jars are closed and either stored in a refrigerator (won't work for us!) or processed in a hot water bath or pressure cooker.

Photo credit: Behan Gifford

Home-canned veggies are delicious—a wonderful treat
to take along if you're heading to remote areas.

See our recipe for pickling carrots in Appendix B – it can be adapted
for many other vegetables, too. And you can find a lot of good pickling
recipes online—the main variants are the spices and the combination of
vegetables used. I particularly like the instruction booklet and recipes put
out by the Oregon State University extension office. Refer to my section
on canning meat (page 7) for a great way to store glass jars on a boat.

I had never really thought of pickling as simply a way to give a
different taste to canned vegetables until pre-publication reader John
Herlig mentioned it. He has cruised for years without refrigeration and
doesn't really like canned vegetables, but sometimes they're the only
choice. So he pickles foods such as canned corn, green beans, carrots and
fresh red onions as well as canned black and pinto beans. His "recipe"
is in Appendix B. He notes that the sweet/starchy foods such as corn,
black beans, and pinto beans will only last a couple of days without
refrigeration; green beans a week; and red onions several weeks.

Kimchi

Kimchi is a Korean way to ferment cabbage for storage. It's very spicy and a little on the salty side, but typically is eaten in small portions as a way to spice up other bland foods. If you don't like really spicy food, don't despair: you can tone down the amount of pepper used! It provides a lot of Vitamins A and C, as well as probiotics and antioxidants.

Kimchi is great as a condiment on eggs, tofu, or rice, and I love a bit on top of a grilled or sautéed fish fillet. Kimchi will last about a week without refrigeration (after its fermentation time)—longer if it's cool out. If it begins to pick up some mold—visible or by taste—it's time to pitch it.

Find our kimchi recipe in Appendix B.

You can use the same basic recipe to ferment green, red or Napa cabbage, carrots, cucumbers, green beans, kohlrabi, or zucchini.

Grow Your Own

One popular way to have fresh greens, sprouts, and herbs without refrigeration is to grow your own. I've known several cruisers who keep pots in the cockpit at anchor and move them into the sink when underway; RVing friends tell me they do the same. Just pick what you need at meal time!

Basil is a favorite and quite tolerant of conditions. Other good ones include oregano, rosemary, cilantro, sage, tarragon, and thyme. If you are in a cool climate, it's possible to grow your own lettuce too, although it takes a fair amount of space to grow enough for more than a single salad.

If you have a sufficient water supply, growing sprouts is a good way to add fresh greens and crunch to your meals. And really, the water usage isn't as bad as you might think, as you can re-use the rinse water from the sprouts in other cooking—and it's filled with nutrients. Do not use water that smells of chlorine—it will kill the seeds/sprouts. If you recently treated your water with chlorine and don't have a charcoal filter to remove it, pour water into a pan or bowl and let it sit for several hours until the chlorine dissipates.

You'll need a container (glass or plastic), a piece of clean cloth, a string or rubber band, sprouting seeds, and water. The type of container isn't really important—even an old water or soda bottle will work as long as it's clean. If you use a bottle with a narrow neck, make sure it's something that you're willing to cut up to get the sprouts out. You can buy special sprouting jars with easy-drain lids, but they are not necessary.

The nice thing is that seeds take up relatively little space and can be

stored almost anywhere that is cool and dry, even in those little nooks and crannies where nothing ever fits. Each pound (half kilo) of seeds will produce about eight pounds (3.6 kilos) of sprouts—or four times the volume!

Almost any vegetable seeds can be used for sprouts, but the most popular are:

- Alfalfa
- Beans (pretty much all varieties, not only the popular mung beans)
- Broccoli (does best in cool weather)
- Celery
- Dill
- Chia
- Clover
- Fenugreek

Adding homegrown sprouts to the top of a salad made from canned goods adds crunch as well as nutrients.

- Grains (wheat, oats, quinoa, millet, almost anything)
- Lentils
- Garlic
- Peas
- Radish
- Kale
- Onion (including red and green)
- Pumpkin
- Sesame
- Sunflower

Seed mixtures are great: you can either buy a premade mix or simply mix and match your own to get just the taste you want. It's best to buy seeds intended for sprouting; definitely buy seeds that have not been treated with any type of pesticide or insecticide and rinse them thoroughly before beginning the sprouting process. My favorite source for seeds and detailed information on sprouting all sorts of mixtures is Sprout People.

Growing sprouts is easy and doesn't even require sunlight. Start by rinsing seeds to get any dirt or contamination off. Fill your sprouting jar no more than one-quarter full of seeds (they'll expand considerably). Cover with at least two inches (5 cm) of water. Place cheesecloth or light cloth over the top and secure it with a rubber band or piece of string tied around it. Let soak eight to twelve hours.

Drain the seeds by turning the jar upside down and letting the cloth over the top act as a filter. Add water to cover the seeds and then drain again. Place the jar on a 45° angle with the top down, so that water continues to drain. Putting it on angle in a bowl tends to work well as the bowl collects any water.

Various directions I've read say to keep the sprouting seeds in a cool place, out of direct sunlight. Frankly, that hasn't always been possible.

Outside of some seed mixtures that specifically said they did best in cool climates, I haven't had a problem as long as (a) the feels-like temperature stayed under 100^0 F and (b) I was able to rinse and drain often enough that the soon-to-be-sprouts didn't totally dry out. The feels-like temperature, or heat index, is a combination of heat and humidity and I find it a better predictor of whether my seeds will do well or just rot than going strictly by temperature.

Keep rinsing and draining the seeds anywhere from two to four times a day until the seeds sprout. This can take anywhere from one day to five days, depending on the type of seeds. The seed package will usually tell how long to expect it to take. Really, though, it's a matter of personal preference: taste the sprouts at each rinse and stop when you like the taste and texture!

Give them one final rinse and put into a colander or strainer. Pick any loose hulls or unsprouted seeds out, then leave the sprouts to dry another eight to ten hours. Once dry, place in a bowl to store and cover with cheesecloth or other light cloth—do not use plastic wrap or a plastic bag as the covering must let air through.

Most sprouts will last close to a week without refrigeration if well-drained and put in a ventilated bowl (put cheesecloth or a very light cloth over it to keep dust and bugs out). Again, the higher the heat index, the fewer days they'll last. I prefer to make smaller batches and start them every couple of days so that I'm not trying to keep them too long. Fresh are definitely better!

Dehydrated Vegetables

Dehydrated veggies can be a good backup supply for times when you can't resupply with fresh. To me, dehydrated foods are best used to fill in what's not available in canned. That's not to say that you can't use dehydrated for everything, just that dishes will generally be best with fresh, better with canned and okay with dehydrated.

Dehydrated vegetables are lighter weight than canned, can be used in any amount (versus opening a whole can for a few tablespoons) and store in less space. The disadvantages are that the foods are generally in small pieces (peas and corn kernels are whole; most other veggies are in 1/4" dices, which leads to blobby meals if they are the only vegetables) and require extra water to reconstitute. They also cost more per serving.

The "needing water" aspect of dehydrated vegetables shouldn't be overlooked if you have limited water available. The increase won't be huge, but canned vegetables and fruit have the advantage of coming with extra liquid that can be used in cooking to reduce the other water used. Of course, that means that they weigh considerably more—instead of carrying water in your tanks, you're carrying it in cans.

Dehydrated onions, leeks, shallots, sweet and hot peppers, and celery are quite good in my opinion, particularly when you just need a little in a recipe. Peas and sweet corn are good as add-ins to recipes but not great on their own. Zucchini and sweet potatoes make good bread and muffins. Other veggies are less satisfactory due to being chopped so finely.

Thrive brand is excellent but comes in hard-to-store large cans. Not only do the cans waste storage space, but I find the can sizes to be too large to be practical for two people.

Harmony House products are good and come in a variety of package sizes, with the medium and large sizes coming in squared off plastic jars that pack tightly (see photo above of the medium size); the smallest containers are vacuum-sealed bags that are easy to tuck into odd places. The small pouches and medium-size (quart/liter) jars are good for up to about four people; because I use green beans as the base for many salads, I buy those in the large (gallon) container.

Dishes made primarily from dehydrated food tastes just fine, but tend to resemble one another as a "stew-y" mash, just with different flavors. It's best to prepare dehydrated foods as soups, stews, and casserole-type dishes. You cannot sauté or brown any of the foods.

The tomato powder is a good substitute for tomato sauce and paste. You can make very good spaghetti sauce with it. However, it picks up moisture very easily and becomes hard in its jar—it's not horrible to break up initially but after several months it will be rock hard; keeping some dried beans in the jar will help. A medium jar of tomato powder is a LOT for two people; considering the problem with the powder absorbing moisture, it's better to get a couple of the small pouches so that you finish one before it gets too hard.

Dehydrated celery is good for flavor, but not for adding crunch. Jalapenos are great for adding a bit of zip. Six ounces (a quart/liter jar)

Heading to an out-of-the-way spot where you don't know what vegetables you'll be able to find? Dehydrated veggies take up very little space but don't quite have the texture or taste of fresh or canned. However, they are MUCH better than nothing!

of dried jalapenos goes a long ways, even if you like Cajun and Mexican food.

The green beans are absolutely excellent, although they're also cut short. Green beans and corn are the two veggies that are good just by themselves. As noted above, I also used rehydrated green beans extensively as the base for salads (see recipe for Green Bean Salad in Appendix B).

The zucchini, sweet potatoes, and butternut squash all worked well in my recipe for zucchini bread (Appendix B), and I often made this the day before we were getting underway at dawn—we'd have a piece of the bread for breakfast or a snack.

The soup mixes were great and nice when we needed a quick meal, especially if I had some homemade bread to go along with it. I'd boil the soup mix with water, bouillon and other spices, and add some meat just before serving.

There are no spices or salt in any of the dehydrated or freeze-dried foods, and I soon learned to add a bit more spice than I did when using canned food. Spices go a long way in improving the taste of meals made substantially with dehydrated food.

Dehydrating your own is an option that many people ask about. The biggest problem is that it is almost impossible to get foods as uniformly dry as commercial processing, and thus the foods have a greater tendency to mold when stored for any length of time in a hot or humid environment. Part of this can also be attributed to the fact that commercial dehydrators chop the food finely. If we dehydrate the food ourselves, we can make larger pieces, but they don't dry as completely or as consistently. A great deal of the practicality of doing it yourself depends on two things: do you have the space to store and use a dehydrator, and are you making short trips where food will be used before it molds? For me, it has been much more practical to buy commercial products.

Dried Fruit

Dried fruit such as raisins, dates, cranberries, apricots, blueberries, and more can be found in almost any grocery store. Dried fruits are tasty and nutritious and just what many of us eat anyway. They require no special handling or storage other than to put them in an airtight container after opening. My experience is that commercial dried and packaged products last much, much longer than home-dried, especially in hot and humid climates.

Herbs & Spices

Admittedly, you can get virtually any herb or spice in a jar, so storing them without refrigeration isn't a necessity. The nice thing is that most fresh herbs are pretty easy to store—just place them in a glass of water as if you had cut flowers. Replace the water every few days and be sure to secure the glass underway. If you have green onions that you are storing in a glass of water, you can put the herbs in the same glass if there is room.

I've had great luck storing fresh ginger
by doing absolutely nothing special to it!

Fresh ginger is even easier to store. While most of us have been taught to freeze it, it's fine just left out at room temperature. It may even start to grow, yes, without soil or anything! Just cut or break off a piece whenever you need it.

Fresh garlic that is commercially sold will last months when stored in a cool, dry place. Do not store in plastic or anything that will trap humidity and moisture as that will cause it to either sprout or rot. It does not have to be kept in the dark—ventilation is more important. If buying fresh garlic at a farmer's market, look to see if has been "cured" or allowed to dry. You can tell cured garlic as the outer skin is dry and the tops are brown or have fallen off. Green tops mean that the garlic is not fully cured and will only last a few weeks.

Milk

Milk seems impossible to have without refrigeration (or a cow!) and yet turns out to be one of the easiest to handle with the advent of the Tetra Pak and truly good powdered milk. Whether you prefer whole, skim, soy, almond, or any other variety of milk, there are options for you.

Just a few years ago, boxed milk was difficult to find in many stores. As this May 2018 photo shows, it's now fairly easy to find boxed regular milk as well as soy, rice, hemp, and almond milk.

Boxed Milk of All Types

Boxed milk—ultra-pasteurized and packaged in Tetra Paks (aka juice packs)—is wonderful when you don't have refrigeration. It will last months, unopened, at room temperature. The only time it needs to be refrigerated is after it is opened, and this can be managed by buying smaller packages.

You can usually get cow's milk (whole, skim, 2%), soy milk, almond milk, and rice milk in boxes.[1]

From here on, I'll refer to all types generically as "milk" unless a comment only applies to certain types. However, as with anything, there are differences between brands and you may like one more than another. Buy one and try it before buying a case!

If you have a cooler where you can keep opened boxes of milk (or have a large number of people), the quart boxes are a better value. Otherwise, the single-serving boxes are best as you won't waste part of each box.

Each single-serving box contains one cup (250 ml) of milk—a generous amount for one bowl of cereal or two somewhat skimpy bowls. We generally allow one per person and drink any that we don't use on our cereal (if you take milk in your coffee, that is a good use for the extra).

Depending on where you shop, boxed milk may be prominent-ly displayed or almost impossible to locate. I've found it in the baking aisle, with coffee, with juice, with cereal, near the refrigerated milk, and once in the candy aisle! Often, the quarts and single-serving boxes are in different places.

Most of the single-serving boxes are intended for kids to take in school lunches and often come in strawberry and chocolate as well as plain or vanilla. Vanilla is usually an okay choice for cereal and baking when you can't find plain. I have almost always found the single servings in 4-packs.

---

1   I've never seen boxed buttermilk; chocolate milk is not common but is seen more often.

Since they're intended for kids, the single-serving boxes come with a straw and a little foil place to stick the straw in. Rather than piercing the foil and trying to pour the milk out of the ragged hole, I've learned to find an edge of the foil and just peel the whole thing off. This gives you a smooth hole to pour from without it going everywhere.

The one downside of boxed milk is that Tetra Paks are recyclable only in locations with high-tech carton recycling facilities and should not be burned either. They have a layer of plastic sandwiched between cardboard and foil—if you try to burn the packages, the foil won't burn, and the plastic will emit toxic smoke. Take care to dispose of them properly!

Evaporated Milk

Evaporated milk might be called old-fashioned shelf-stable milk. It comes in cans and is usually found in the baking aisle. To use as milk,

Rather than piercing the foil, pull it off
and the milk will pour without dribbling.

you mix it with water. It is not nearly as good as the other alternatives discussed in this chapter.

Powdered Milk

No, I'm not suggesting drinking powdered milk on a regular basis. I much prefer boxed milk for drinking, cereal, and things like that. However, powdered milk—that is, good powdered milk—works wonderfully to make your own yogurt (see page 130), and in baking, mashed potatoes, and other dishes. It also takes up a lot less space, weighs far less than boxed milk, and lasts almost forever. It doesn't have to be refrigerated until mixed with water, either!

If your only experience with powdered milk is Carnation nonfat milk or a generic equivalent sold in most baking aisles, you're in for a real treat when you try some of the other brands. Powdered milk really can be good.

Go over to the Latin, Mexican, or International foods aisle (rarely, you'll find the good stuff with the other powdered and boxed milk). Look for "instant" whole (full cream) powdered milk, usually sold in cans. Sometimes there will be more than one variety, with some

Yes, there really is good powdered milk.
It just comes from other countries.

containing additives such as added fat, prebiotics, and/or flavorings. In general, the fewer additives the better. Almost all have added vitamins and soy lecithin—these don't cause any problems in cooking or baking.

Brands known for excellent quality include:

- Nido or Klim, from Mexico. The best of each of these is the fortificado option. The kind with extra fat and additives will not culture to make yogurt.

- Anchor, from New Zealand

- New Zealand, from New Zealand

- Peak, from Holland

Most stores will only carry one of these brands. You can also buy them from Amazon and other online sources, which also carry a number of other brands of powdered whole milk. Before buying one of these other brands, read reviews and mixing directions carefully—one key to finding the really good brands is that they dissolve almost instantly. Stay away from ones that suggest they sit overnight before serving.

Powdered Buttermilk

You can buy powdered buttermilk in the baking aisle of most groceries and also online. It is good in recipes, but is not particularly good for drinking. If you don't use it often enough to justify carrying it, you can substitute yogurt in an equal measurement, use half yogurt and half milk, or use all milk plus 1 teaspoon (5 ml) white vinegar per ¼ cup (60 ml) of milk.

Powdered Coconut Milk

Just as this book was going to press, I found powdered coconut milk in my local store. It's much lighter and easier to carry than cans. It worked well in a coconut-curry sauce and in baking. It helps if you have some coconut oil to add to it—I replaced about two tablespoons (30 ml) of the recommended water amount per cup (250 ml) of reconstituted coconut milk. I wouldn't really recommend it for drinking or cereal.

Powdered buttermilk can be found in almost all stores. Be sure to put the cardboard package inside a Ziploc or it will pick up moisture from the air and go moldy in a few months.

Powdered Soy Milk

I've tried several brands of powdered soy milk and have not found one that we like the taste of, even in baking.

Yogurt

People have been eating yogurt and its precursors for about 8,000 years—in other words, long before there was refrigeration. The trick is to make your own yogurt from good powdered milk and make just enough for a day (if you don't have a cooler) or two days (if you do). If you like eating yogurt every day, it's easy to keep it going by using a bit of the last batch as starter for the next batch.

A good idea is to get packets of starter online so that you can start up again if you let it die out. You do not have to use a new starter pack every day; only when you don't have any left from your previous batch. Packets of freeze-dried starter tend to be on the expensive side, but you don't have to commit to making and eating it every day.

I buy Yogourmet starter culture; it does not require refrigerating or freezing the packets if they are not used at once, as some do. I do not use an electric yogurt maker but rather make it in a Thermos bottle and follow my own recipe, which you can find in Appendix B (see page 130), rather than the package directions.

Cream

While I prefer the alternatives in this chapter, there are times that powdered creams make sense (see page 87). I use a variety of cream options for the best flavor.

Media Crema (Table Cream)

Media crema is half-and-half or light cream that comes in a can or box. It's much more popular in Latin America and Caribbean nations and is considered an international food in the US, where you'll find it in the Latin foods aisle of most grocery stores, or in a Mexican grocery. It is not the same thing as sweetened condensed milk or evaporated milk.

Homemade yogurt is easy and delicious—especially if you've just been provisioning and have some fresh berries. Other good no-refrigeration toppings are granola, honey, and dried or canned fruit.

Media crema (literally "half cream") typically comes in eight-ounce (250 ml; 1 cup) cans and Tetra Paks. Unopened, it will last six months to one year without refrigeration, but once opened, any unused portion does need to be kept in a cooler. Shake it well before opening as the solids in the cream will settle.

Lots of non-refrigerated dishes are just so much better when made with media crema instead of milk:

- Clam, fish or seafood chowder—either with freshly caught seafood or canned
- Potato soup with ham or bacon
- Macaroni and cheese
- Fettuccine Alfredo
- Scalloped potatoes/potatoes au gratin
- Cream and cheese sauces for pasta and veggies

Media crema or table cream is made by several different companies and can be found in most grocery stores—but often takes a bit of searching to find it.

- Quiche

With media crema on hand, you can have real sour cream without refrigeration (see page 74). Great for appetizers!

The only bad side to media crema is the fat and calories. Yes, unfortunately, it is just like using cream. If you're looking for a lower fat option, use undiluted evaporated milk—it also comes in a can, is a little richer than milk and will last nearly forever. It's not nearly as thick and rich as media crema, though, and you can't make sour cream from evaporated milk.

Coffee Cream

If you take cream in your coffee and are not a fan of Coffee Mate, try a spoonful of one of the good powdered milks, above. You can also use media crema, discussed above. It's wonderful and rich, but each can contains about one cup (250 ml) of cream, so you'll need a cooler (and securely lidded container!) to store the unused portion in.

Another option is "Mini-Moos" which are single-serving packages of ultra-pasteurized real cream that do not have to be refrigerated. They are a huge step above the non-dairy creamer packaged almost identically that you may be more used to. The downside to the Mini-Moos is the amount of storage space that they take up and the amount of trash that they generate. Mini-Moos tend to be available at wholesale clubs and not grocery stores, although I have occasionally seen them in standard supermarkets; you can also buy them online.

Whipping Cream

Media crema is wonderful and relatively easy to find, but the one disadvantage is that it won't whip up.

In the US, however, you can get UHT boxed whipping cream at Trader Joe's[2], and you can buy the Trader Joe's brand online if you don't have a store near you. Canadian readers have told me that once in a while

---

2   I've never seen or heard of another brand of shelf-stable whipping cream sold in the US.

they find various brands of canned whipping cream in supermarkets, too. Unopened packages will last six months or longer and can be stored almost anywhere.

The Trader Joe's package recommends chilling for six hours before whipping. If you don't have a cooler to chill it, it will still whip up, but

won't have quite as much volume. It's hard to make whipped cream with a whisk, but an old-fashioned hand-crank egg beater does a great job. An immersion blender is even better.

Because it is ultra-pasteurized, the boxed whipping cream does not beat up quite as high as refrigerated whipping cream and loses it's "fluff" more quickly. It's best to whip it up just before using and eat it all.

Sour Cream

Commercial sour cream turns green in a day without refrigeration and doesn't last much longer even with a cooler. But if you have media crema on hand, you can have sour cream whenever you want it.

Sour cream is extremely easy to make:

- Put the contents of an eight-ounce (250 ml) can or box of

media crema in a lidded plastic container. Be sure to scrape the thick cream out of the can or box.

• Add 2 teaspoons (10 ml) of vinegar (you won't taste it if you use white vinegar, other types are very slightly noticeable), lemon juice, lime juice, or white wine.

• Mix thoroughly. As you stir, it will thicken.

Use the sour cream immediately if you do not have a cooler. If you have a cooler, put the lid on and chill for a half hour or more before using. Chilling will make it even thicker.

Use it in any recipe, just as you would any other sour cream. It makes great dips and garnishes. Note that this makes 1 cup (a half pint/250 ml)—many dip recipes call for a pint (half liter), so you'd need a double batch.

If you only need a bit of sour cream flavor, you can use sour cream powder which is discussed on page 87.

Butter or Margarine

If you have sufficient space in a cooler, you can keep butter or margarine there. I'll refer to both as "butter" in this chapter except when a particular comment applies to only one. Use a gasketed locking plastic container, such as a Lock & Lock. You can tuck it anywhere, including right into the ice or in a secondary cooler that uses the cool melt water from your primary cooler. Good gasketed storage containers are watertight, so you don't have to worry about dirty water coming into contact with the butter.

Assuming that you can't keep butter in a cooler or tiny refrigerator, I'll discuss five alternatives in this chapter:
- Room temperature storage
- Canned butter
- Butter bell
- Brining butter
- Butter substitutes

Butter tends to "go bad" in one of two ways: either becoming rancid or moldy. Rancid butter will both smell and taste off. If the butter smells sour or bitter when you open the container, it's rancid and should be discarded. You may notice moldy butter by taste before it's obvious to the eye: a quick sniff before using is the best test to avoid eating it. Don't worry if you do eat a bit of it, though; small quantities are unlikely to make you sick.

Storing Butter at Room Temperature

If the weather is cool, you can store butter or margarine at room temperature for a surprising length of time. Again, put it in a gasketed locking plastic container so that if the temperature warms up and the butter softens, it will not leak out. This type of container will also prevent bugs from getting in. Keep the container in a dark location—wrapping it with paper, a bag, or even a dish towel is sufficient.

How long butter will keep without refrigeration depends on several factors:

- How hot it is. The warmer it is, the sooner butter will turn rancid. I have had butter last as long as four days when temperatures were above 90° F (32° C), but I wouldn't count on it lasting that long—typically just a day or two. It will last longer at cooler temperatures, all else being the same. Butter will be soft with temperatures above 80° F (26° C) and runny in the 90's. Butter— as long as it's not contaminated with food bits—will last several weeks if temperatures are in the 60's or 70's (15 – 25° C) and even longer if cooler.
- Keeping butter in a dark location (such as wrapping the container with a cloth or a bag) will add a few days to its life if temperatures are under 80° F.
- Salt is a preservative, and salted butter will stay good longer than unsalted.
- Contaminating butter with toast crumbs or other food by reusing a knife sets up a favorable environment for mold. Wiping off a utensil before using it in the butter container noticeably improves the storage time.
- For margarine, shelf life is also variable by brand.

Canned Butter

Commercially-canned butter will provide you with a way to keep more butter on hand. Most cans contain twelve ounces of butter— equivalent to three sticks in the US or about 350 ml for those using metric measurements. Unopened, most brands are shelf-stable for several years—the only problem is that it will get soft to runny when stored in warm places and can even separate. If it is hot out, you have to find the coolest possible place to store it if you want your canned butter to stay a solid.

Once you open a can, store the butter as any other in a cooler, at room temperature, in a butter bell, or brined. You can buy canned butter online; most is imported from New Zealand and absolutely delicious. Red Feather is a popular brand and available online. I have never seen canned margarine, though, only real butter.

Butter Bell

A butter bell will let you store butter for a longer time at room temperature. A butter bell has a porcelain top that typically holds one-half cup of butter (one US stick or 120 g). This fits upside-down into a slightly larger porcelain bottom that you fill with cool water. The porcelain and cool water insulate and seal the butter and will keep it fresh for up to one month; longer in cool weather. All you have to do is change the water every few days.

Always use a clean utensil to get butter out of the bell; little bits of bread or other food can start mold forming. There are many butter bells for sale online; the highly-rated inexpensive ones work just as well as the expensive ones.

A butter bell can only do so much, though. There are three potential problems with a butter bell:

- The hotter the ambient temperature, the more likely the butter is to slide right out of the top of the butter bell. Once temperatures get into the low 90's (above 32° C), a butter bell just won't work.
- They hold a relatively small amount if you're traveling for several weeks to months.
- You have to find a secure place to store the butter bell since porcelain can break.

A couple of times, I've had to improvise a butter bell to store some extra butter. I've packed the butter into a gasketed, locking plastic container (no more than three-quarters full), then filled it with cool water—right over the butter—and put the lid on. This works best when temperatures are below 80° F (26° C) and the butter isn't getting too soft. Even with firm butter, a little water will stick to it as you get it out to use it. I change water daily and add more water as I use the butter so that the container stays full.

I use the butter from this makeshift bell first as a real butter bell keeps it fresh longer.

Brining Butter

One of the "rough draft" readers of this book was John Herlig, who has cruised for four years with no refrigeration.

He told me how he brines butter to store it for up to four months:

1. Make a brine with eight parts of water to one of un-iodized salt, heat it enough for the salt to fully dissolve and let it cool overnight.

8-ounce jars of brined butter, ready to go into the bilge.

2. In boiling water, sterilize enough canning jars to hold the butter and let them sit, upside-down on towels, overnight to cool. Once sterilized, don't touch the inside of the jars with your hand or anything else that is not sterilized. The small 4- and 8-ounce jars work best for butter; others are too large unless you have a very large group of people.

3. If butter is rock hard from the store, let it soften a bit, but do not let it melt.

4. Pack butter (using boiled, sterilized utensils) into the sterilized jars and pour the cooled brine over the top, making sure it has a path down to any air pockets visible below the top and completely covering the butter.

5. Screw the lid on, drop into a sock or roll in bubble wrap, and place them in the coolest storage areas you have (he puts them in the bilge of Ave del Mar).

6. Use clean utensils to remove the butter.

7. After removing what you want, top up the jar with fresh water as

needed so that the butter remains covered.

As with all other methods of storing butter without refrigeration, if it gets too warm where the butter is stored, the butter is unlikely to be usable. It will melt and form an unappetizing goo with the brine.

Substitutes for Butter

There are several things you can do to cut down on the amount of butter you need to be able to store and avoid butter totally when it's too hot to store without refrigeration. Use:

- Olive oil dips for bread
- Peanut butter or jelly on toast and bagels
- Canola, vegetable, or olive oil for most cooking and baking needs
- Sour cream on baked potatoes

Another option is ghee, which is clarified butter. It is most often used in Indian and Southeast Asian dishes, but there is no reason it can't be used in other recipes. The milk solids have been removed from it, so it has a different texture and taste from butter, but is still very good.

Unopened commercial jars and cans of ghee are good for years (typically at least ten) and opened jars are generally good for at least three months without refrigeration as long as they are not contaminated. You can buy commercially prepared ghee in Indian grocery stores and online. You can also make your own, although it is unlikely to last as long as commercially prepared.

Cheese

Cheese was one of the ways that milk was preserved long before there was refrigeration. Most cheeses are labelled "Keep Refrigerated" and, of course, that is the safest course of action.

The FDA recommends that only hard cheese encased in wax be kept without refrigeration; there are risks of food-borne illness. Cheeses made from unpasteurized milk carry much greater risk. Young children, pregnant or nursing women, or anyone who is sick or has a compromised immune system should be extra cautious in eating non-refrigerated cheese.

I store cheese without refrigeration, but your decision to do so is yours and at your own risk. There are far too many variables for me to guarantee that you will be safe doing the same. If you have a weakened immune system or other health concerns, you may not want to store cheese without refrigeration; botulism and listeria are the two primary concerns beyond simple mold.

The best cheeses for storage without refrigeration are those encased in wax or vacuum-sealed in plastic. The harder the cheese, the better it will last without refrigeration.

Research[1] has shown that several types of hard cheeses generally are safe to be stored without refrigeration:

- Asiago (medium and aged)
- Aged Cheddar
- Colby
- Feta
- Monterey Jack
- Muenster
- Parmesan
- Pasteurized Process Cheese
- Provolone
- Romano
- Swiss

Yes, it's possible to have cheese without refrigeration.

---

1   http://www.cheesesociety.org/wp-content/uploads/2013/07/2013_Safe_Cheese_Storage_Smukowski.pdf

Cheddar in wax is one of the best cheeses for storing without refrigeration. Sometimes I can find very small waxed wheels (Babybel brand is most common) that are wonderful as they can be eaten in a single meal or snack. Vacuum-sealed cheese sticks are also good. I've eaten week-old cheddar sticks that weren't refrigerated; I've never had occasion to try to keep them longer.

Shredded or crumbled cheese does very poorly without refrigeration— you are better off getting and storing a block of cheese and crumbling or grating it yourself when you need it. Soft cheeses such as mozzarella, cream cheese, and cottage cheese also do poorly and are much more susceptible to bacterial contamination. Ricotta is easy to make yourself from powdered milk, but must be eaten the same day if you do not have a cooler (see Appendix B, page 157, for a recipe to make your own ricotta).

Place waxed cheeses in zipper plastic bags or vacuum seal them for the longest storage. Even wrapping in aluminum foil will add to the shelf life. Unopened waxed cheeses will last one month or more, even in tropical temperatures. The cheese may get a little oily, and the texture may change slightly, but the cheese is still good to eat.

Cheeses that have a rind, such as Brie and Camembert, should be covered with waxed paper or cheesecloth. If it's cool, they'll last several weeks unopened; if it's over about 70° F (21° C), the shelf life is progressively shorter, down to just days when it's over 90° F (32° C). Once opened, these cheeses need to be eaten at once if the unused portion cannot be put into a cooler; even with a cooler, they will only last three or four days before becoming moldy.

To store cheeses not in wax and waxed/rind cheeses once cut, wipe the cut surfaces with white vinegar. Then wrap the cheese in waxed paper, cheesecloth (best), or even a paper towel and store it in the coolest place you can. Depending on where you're going to store it, you can place the cheese and wrap in a plastic container.

The vinegar will help prevent mold, but if the cheese does pick up a bit of mold, you can simply cut it off and the wipe again with vinegar.

Feta does very well when packed into small sterilized canning jars and covered with olive oil. Follow the instructions for brining butter (see page 79), using plain olive oil instead of brine and water. It will last two to four weeks, depending on the temperature. Do NOT add other ingredients—garlic and sun-dried tomatoes are popular—when storing without refrigeration as this increases the risk of botulism.

Cheddar also does well in olive oil. I cut it into "sticks" about one inch by one inch and slightly shorter than the fill line on my jars. Pack the sticks in the jars and cover with olive oil the same way. It will last up to two months if kept cool.

For both feta and cheddar packed in olive oil, the jars need to be padded with rags, tube socks, or bubble wrap. It's also a good idea to pack them—upright—into a plastic bin. Olive oil is susceptible to oozing out of the jar threads just slightly as the boat or vehicle moves, so it's a good idea to check periodically and wipe any drips up.

As with butter, you can find canned cheese (real cheese, not Cheez Whiz type products) in some locations. Canned cheese has a very long shelf life—the manufacturer says indefinite—before it's opened. Here in the US, the most popular brand is Bega mild cheddar cheese, imported from Australia. You can buy it from many online retailers; cans contain about a half pound. Once opened, store any uneaten portion as described above.

Powdered Cream, Sour Cream, Cheese and Butter

If you search online for shelf-stable dairy products, you'll quickly discover several brands selling a wide variety of powdered products, including powdered cream, sour cream, cheese, and butter. Most sell good powdered milk and eggs, too, but I prefer the brands I discuss in the respective chapters as having still better taste and texture.

Think of the powdered cheese, butter, sour cream, and so on as flavorings, not substitutes for the texture and substance of the real thing (the alternatives discussed in previous chapters do substitute well for the real thing). The best way to describe the difference is to compare Kraft Macaroni & Cheese made with the cheese powder to mac & cheese made with real cheese or Velveeta. And you certainly wouldn't want cheese powder on a cracker in place of a cheese slice!

Powders work well in soups, salad dressings, and other recipes. My experience is that the powdered cream and sour cream do not reconstitute well into a stand-alone product; you're much better off with the alternatives I've discussed previously. But to say add a bit of sour cream flavor to potato soup? Yes, the powdered sour cream is great for that.

You can find many powdered products online and in stores geared towards preppers, but they are almost always in one-pound or larger quantities. This poses a problem for many of us on boats or camping: it's simply more than we need, not to mention the storage space the container will take up.

Further, while most of these can be stored for six months to one year unopened, they don't last long once opened if you can't keep them in a cool location. Most brands/products recommend that the unused portion be refrigerated. Depending on the product, they'll get moldy, sour, or rancid.

Without refrigeration, I prefer to buy small containers even though they cost more per ounce; they are cheaper overall as I can use up items before they go bad. The Savory Spice Shop has a wide variety of good powdered products in small containers—both glass bottles and plastic bags. The glass bottles are more airtight but take more space to store. You do have to consider possible breakage, but the bottles are tough.

Eggs

Being able to have eggs without refrigeration is huge as far as expanding the meals you can have. Baked goods, breakfasts, and even boiled eggs for salads and snacks are suddenly back on the menu.

Cardboard egg cartons may be more environmentally friendly, but sometimes bugs will nest in them. Styrofoam cartons can be washed out with bleach water and reused numerous times if you buy loose eggs at a farmer's market.

Unrefrigerated Eggs

Unrefrigerated whole eggs are a staple for those living or traveling without refrigeration. Much of the world does not refrigerate eggs, but in the US, the FDA cautions against it. The main risk is salmonella, which can enter through microscopic cracks in the shell. Thoroughly cooking eggs will reduce the risk, but if you are concerned, you can opt to use powdered eggs instead (see the next section for good powdered eggs).

I store eggs without refrigeration, but your decision to do so is yours and at your own risk. There are far too many variables for me to guarantee that you will be safe doing the same. If you have a weakened immune system or other health concerns, I urge you to use powdered eggs instead.

Eggs that have never been refrigerated are best for continuing to store without refrigeration. For years I thought that, once refrigerated, eggs had to be kept refrigerated. I've since heard from several people who take eggs that were refrigerated at the store and keep them without refrigeration and have now done it for over four years myself.

Simply store the eggs in a cool and protected location, either in a carton or padded bin. While some people say to coat the egg shells with petroleum jelly to keep bacteria out, I have never done this and most people I know don't. It's extra work and attracts dirt, and the egg is slippery when you go to pick it up! If eggs were previously refrigerated, let them sit for several hours to come up to room temperature, then wipe any condensation off. This will greatly decrease the chance of mold on the shells.

Every day or two, flip the carton over so that the membrane on the inside stays moist. This helps block any bacteria from reaching the inside. Never use an egg with a visible crack in the shell.

I have been able to store eggs without refrigeration for one month, sometimes longer. When I use the eggs, I crack them into a cup individually—if bad, you will smell it instantly, there is no doubt about it—and then transfer to whatever I'm making. In over fifteen years of using unrefrigerated eggs, I've only had two that were bad. NOTE: this is not a test for salmonella, but whether the egg has gone rotten.

The other test for whether an egg is good (again, not for salmonella) is to put the whole egg (still in its shell) into a glass of fresh water. If the egg sinks and lies on its side, it's very fresh. If it lies on an angle, it's fresh. If it stands on end with one end on the bottom, it's still good but should be used reasonably soon. And if it floats, it's bad—don't crack it

A bad egg. Don't crack it—it is rotten and will smell horribly.

as it will stink.

If you break an egg and notice that the sac encasing the yolk is disintegrating (which happens as it ages), it's still fine to use the egg if it doesn't stink. You can't use it for a fried egg, but it's fine for scrambling or using in baking.

Once hard-boiled, eggs shouldn't be kept more than a day without refrigeration whether it is still in the shell or not. Cooking changes the protein and makes them much more susceptible to bacteria.

Powdered Eggs

Do you hear the phrase "powdered eggs" and have visions of watery, tasteless yellow paste from a previous trip? Yep, I've had those and, probably like you, said: "never again."

Guess what? You can now get really good powdered eggs. As with many of the other products I recommend, it's not that all brands are suddenly good. It's a matter of buying the right brand.

OvaEasy powdered eggs actually taste like eggs. You can make scrambled eggs, omelets, quiches, and more. They are simple to use: mix the powder with water, and you can use it immediately just as you would a whole egg (you can also get it as whites-only). About the only thing you can't do with OvaEasy eggs is have a fried, poached, or boiled egg!

They work well in baking and other cooking too—I've learned that they work best if I mix the powder with water and then add the egg to the recipe. I tried a few times to add the egg powder to the dry ingredients and the water to the wet ingredients and the results were not as good.

You can get OvaEasy eggs in pouches that contain the equivalent of a dozen eggs, in large pouches with just over six dozen eggs, and in large

cans sold in two-packs for a total of twelve dozen eggs. I prefer the dozen-egg pouches so that I don't have a huge container open.

The shelf life for OvaEasy eggs ranges from five to seven years unopened (depending on the packaging). Open pouches have a six-month shelf life, although I do put the "open" pouch into an airtight gasketed locking plastic container to keep it from picking up humidity.

We use a combination of unrefrigerated whole eggs and OvaEasy. OvaEasy are lighter weight, aren't subject to breakage, take far less space and care to store, and last even longer. But "regular" eggs are less expensive—and my husband occasionally likes a fried egg for breakfast.

The biggest drawback with OvaEasy eggs is that they are not cheap, recently costing about $0.75 per egg. I have never seen them in a grocery store; I buy them online.

Condiments

Americans are used to having large refrigerators and refrigerate lots of things that people in other countries don't. Most condiments do not need to be refrigerated and do just fine stored at room temperature.

Common Condiments

Let's begin with a list of common foods that do not need to be refrigerated, despite what their packaging may say. Even when I have refrigeration available, I store the following at room temperature:

- Catsup (Ketchup)
- Mustard
- BBQ sauce
- Jam and jelly

- A1
- Worcestershire sauce
- Soy sauce
- Hot sauces, including Sriracha
- Pickles
- Relishes
- Peanut butter
- Chocolate syrup
- Molasses
- Honey

Admittedly, if you keep an opened container long enough, any of these can get moldy, but I've kept them all for months over a tropical summer without them going bad. If you see mold or they smell or taste funny, they should be thrown out.

The Clean Spoon Rule

The most important thing that you can do to keep any condiments from molding is to rigorously follow the clean spoon rule.

Basically, you absolutely never, ever put anything other than a perfectly clean spoon into a condiment container. No wiping a knife on a slice of bread then putting it back in the jar for a second dip. No using the spoon you already used to scrape something out of its can. No taking some out, realizing you took too much, and putting some back. No using a knife that you just sort of wiped off on a rag. Utensils must be clean.

Actually, we prefer to use squeeze bottles and never, ever touch the opening with anything—fingers, food, rags, anything. I'm talking about manufacturer squeeze bottles, not ones that you transfer the products into. The commercial processes are designed to keep contamination out. I also opt for smaller bottles so that we use them up faster.

Horseradish and Wasabi

Horseradish and wasabi won't go bad but will lose their flavor if kept in hot areas, even unopened. It only takes a couple weeks with temperatures over 80° F (26° C) for both to have all the flavor of sawdust. Without refrigeration or a cooler, I don't recommend trying to have either.

Maple Syrup

Once opened, real maple syrup will last about a month without refrigeration and then it will get moldy even if uncontaminated; imitation maple syrup lasts practically forever. If you're like me and prefer the real stuff, buy it in small bottles and use it up quickly. Another option are the tiny bottles available from Jansal Valley—one bottle is perfect for two servings with no leftovers. A good alternative is maple sugar, which will generally last three to six months after opening if kept in a gasketed locked plastic container to keep humidity and ants out (it will pick up mold otherwise).

Mayonnaise and Miracle Whip

Mayonnaise, Miracle Whip, and variations thereon are always the big questions when considering storing food without refrigeration. For this discussion, I'm going to refer to them all generically as mayonnaise. We've all been taught that these are prime suspects for food poisoning, and the FDA says they must be refrigerated after opening.

I don't refrigerate mine—haven't for years—and I know many others who don't. As with unrefrigerated eggs, I can tell you what I do, but you have to make your own decisions. If you decide to store these products without refrigeration, you do so at your own risk.

The clean spoon rule is especially important with mayonnaise-type products to avoid contamination and food poisoning. Squeeze bottles make it much easier, but you still must be careful not to touch the tip to food, your hand, or anything other than an absolutely clean rag (if I have to wipe it off, I use a fresh paper towel to avoid contamination).

Using smaller containers also helps reduce the risk as you're storing each one for less time after it's been opened. Squeeze bottles are generally not large and not a problem; if buying jars, opt for smaller ones unless you have a very large group.

As with all foods, regardless of how they are stored, if it looks funny or smells off, don't eat it. Just dispose of it.

Once you have mixed the mayonnaise into something else—tuna salad, a dip or whatever—it has to be eaten at once or refrigerated. Anything that is not refrigerated and has mayonnaise as an ingredient should be eaten within two hours or disposed of.

Some wonder about making your own mayonnaise as an alternative to storing it at room temperature. You can find many recipes online for making mayonnaise, but once it is made, it must be eaten immediately. It cannot be stored for any length of time without refrigeration. There is always a certain amount of risk with homemade mayo because of the raw eggs; I've always used commercial instead.

If you just can't stomach the thought of unrefrigerated mayonnaise or have a weakened immune system, an alternative is to use single-serving packets of mayonnaise. You can buy them online; sometimes local fast-food restaurants will sell you some as well. A great source of single-serving packets of many foods (not just mayonnaise) is Minimus.biz. Not only is the selection huge, but you can buy exactly how many you want. No more having to buy a thousand at a time!

Bottled Salad Dressings

Bottled salad dressings are another gray area. Many people don't refrigerate them, using the same rules as for mayonnaise. If you use them up fairly quickly, they usually won't get moldy or sour when stored at room temperature. Buying small bottles and only having one type open at a time will help, too. A quick sniff before pouring on your salad is always a good idea.

We simply prefer dressings that I make up shortly before we eat; we rarely buy bottled dressing even when we have refrigeration. Basic vinaigrettes, Greek dressings, and a mayonnaise-based dressing similar to Olive Garden's are our favorites and easy to make (see Appendix B, page 121).

You can also buy single-serving containers of hundreds of commercial dressings on Minimus.biz.

Miscellaneous

If you look in the refrigerator, you'll probably find some other items that I haven't yet talked about; there's not much to say about many of these so I gathered them together here.

Coffee

Coffee actually stores better without refrigeration (condensation is a bigger enemy of flavor than warm temperatures), although you should find a cool and dry spot for it. If you buy coffee in the eight-ounce vacuum-sealed resealable bags, it's best to store the coffee in those, both before and after opening. If storing in an area that could get damp, put the bag in a gasketed locking plastic storage container.

Canned Foods

Canned and jarred foods will last practically forever unopened. A little surface rust will not hurt the contents; cans that are heavily rusted or have rust on the inside should be discarded and the contents not eaten. Once a can is opened, any leftovers generally should be put into a cooler if available.

We try to buy smaller cans or even individual servings of foods we know we are not likely to eat a normal container of all at once. Individual portions of applesauce, peaches, mandarin oranges and olives can be found in most grocery stores and make great snacks.

Juice

Most juice cans, bottles, and boxes can be stored indefinitely unopened. Once opened, most juices won't go bad for a day out of the refrigerator, especially those that have been pasteurized. Still, it's best to buy individual cans or boxes of juices and drink an entire one at a time. You'll find your own favorites, but we've found that we prefer V8 and apple juice when drinking them warm; we're not as wild about warm citrus juices, particularly those that have been pasteurized.

Bouillon and Stock

Most containers of premixed stock have to be refrigerated if you do not use it all at once and thus are a problem when cooking for just one or two people: there's a lot of waste. All bouillon pastes currently available also recommend refrigeration after using, although I have used them without refrigerating but being careful to follow the clean spoon rule. Again, doing so is at your own risk and not recommended for anyone with a compromised immune system.

My second choice are the Knorr powders, available in almost every grocery: the ones in the Mexican foods section have less sodium and are milk-free whereas the ones in the soup aisle have more sodium and contain some milk product (important for those with milk allergies). You can also buy individual packets of concentrated broth in many grocery stores.

Tofu

If you want tofu without refrigeration, you only have one choice as far as I know: Mori-Nu Silken Tofu in Tetra Paks. The important thing to know is that only silken tofu comes in Tetra Paks, and it is softer than regular tofu. Extra firm silken tofu is more like soft regular tofu and must be handled carefully if you want it to be in pieces—it really is more of a pudding consistency than a solid block. It can be used in soups by putting it in a bowl and then pouring the soup around it. It will break apart if you try to put it into the soup pot. It is best for dips and dressings; it is not good for stir fry.

Shelf-stable tofu is a good source of protein, can provide variety in the menu and is relatively inexpensive. Unopened, it will last six to eight months. One twelve-ounce package provides two to three servings.

Leftovers

When living totally without refrigeration or even a cooler, it's best not to have leftovers. If you have a cooler or a small refrigerator and are using the techniques in this book to make the most of what you have, then leftovers are more of a possibility, but still take some special consideration:

- Once foods are combined—as they are in most dishes—they are at much higher risk for harboring bacteria leading to food poisoning. So the fact that something is made from several non-refrigerated ingredients does not mean that an uneaten portion can be stored at room temperature.
- The danger zone for foods breeding bacteria is from 40° F – 135° F (4° C – 57° C). Letting food cool into the danger zone before putting it in the cooler or refrigerator increases the risk of food poisoning. However, putting hot food into a cooler will melt the ice far faster than otherwise; putting it into a small refrigerator will use a lot of electricity to chill it. Neither option is good.

I get questions about whether some spices retard spoilage and food poisoning—there are many urban myths about these, particularly various curries. There are a number of spices that show at least some antimicrobial tendencies, but studies I've read have all indicated that a certain spice inhibited a certain bacteria to a certain extent, but no individual spices or combinations of spices have shown any broad antimicrobial or antibacterial properties sufficient to make leftovers safe without refrigeration.

Some people without refrigeration suggest using a pressure cooker as a giant can: cook something, serve what you want, then bring the pan back up to pressure, turn the burner off and let it sit until the next day. They claim that the pan is sealed, just as a can is. Unfortunately, it's not for two reasons:

- As the pan cools, the pressure inside the pan equalizes to the outside pressure and there is air exchange through the pressure relief valve (these are generally not one-way valves). Never, ever plug the pressure relief valve to try to keep food—it is a major safety device to ensure pressure cookers doesn't blow up!
- As the pan cools and the pressure lessens, the lid is no longer pressed tightly against the seal (this is how you're able to open the pan). It is no longer sealed after as little as ten to twenty minutes.

I do not recommend it, but if you do try to save leftovers without refrigerating them, be sure to bring them to a boil for ten minutes before eating—it takes this long to kill botulism at a full rolling boil.

Cooler

With a cooler and ice, you can take more "fragile" produce, even in tropical temperatures. What's that catsup bottle, you ask? It's got the leftovers from our breakfast box of milk in it—no spillage and fits better down into the ice!

If you have the space and access to ice, you can dramatically extend your food options with a food cooler or ice box. Use a separate cooler from one that you may use for drinks so that the ice will last longer. Plus, while you want to put drinks right down in the ice, that's about the last thing you want for most foods.

Setting Up a Cooler for Food

Rather than placing food directly on the ice—which will melt and you'll end up with your food sitting in water—it's far better to get some racks or grates and put your food in bins on the racks.

Before heading to the store, measure the length and width of your ice box or cooler (I'm just going to call both a "cooler" from now on). If it's not a rectangle, sketch the space and write down the measurements.

Plastic-covered wire "organizers" make easy cooler racks. Racks need to be easily removable to replace ice and clean the box, so don't mount them permanently. The racks don't have to 100% fill the inside of the cooler. They just have to sufficiently fill the space to form a solid base for the bins.

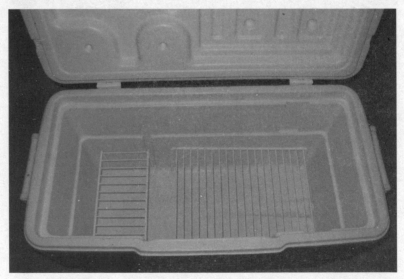

Dry fitting the racks into the cooler. They don't have to cover every single bit of space, but rather simply form a solid base for bins.

Two things are important in choosing your racks:

- You want all the tops to be level, without protrusions that will interfere with your bins.
- You want the racks 5" to 6" (12 to 15 cm.) off the bottom so that sufficient ice can fit under them.

I've used Rubbermaid wire racks that I've found at big box stores; you can find some other brands and sizes at home improvement stores.

If you want a heavier-duty shelf for a large ice box, wire closet shelves are available in most home improvement stores and can be cut to whatever size you need. They are much sturdier if you're trying to span a larger distance.

Also get some bins to hold your food. I like the Sterilite bins, with solid bottoms (less bruising of produce than a ventilated bottom) and ventilated sides (to allow the cold air to circulate).

Think about what you'll want to store in the bins and size them accordingly—for example, if you like celery, you'll need a bin that's big

The Sterilite bins with ventilated sides to let the cool air in,
and solid bottoms to contain anything that might spill,
plus they won't bruise produce with pressure points.

enough for it!

Block ice will last far longer than cubes, although cubes will chill things faster. For food storage, get block ice when you can—it will last five to seven days in a well-insulated ice box even in 90-plus-degree weather (and longer if it's cooler). Cube ice will only last one to two days.

Put the ice under the racks. I find it easiest to put the ice in then put the racks in even when using cube ice. If you are using an ice box that has a drain, leave the drain closed except when you need to drain water out (and it's not a bad thing to have some water around the ice—it's colder than the air). Leaving the drain open will just let hot air into the ice box and constantly remove the cool melt water.

I use the cooler primarily for meat, my more perishable produce and dairy items. Produce and dairy products go in the bins on top. Frozen vacuum-sealed meat packages are tucked into the ice.

If you have a deep ice box, you can also get stacking bins and have a double layer. Put the things that need to stay the coldest on the bottom.

Ice (and melt water) under the racks and food in the bins on top.

Not only are the bottom bins nearest the ice, but hot air rises so it's always warmest at the top.

What to Look For in Buying a Cooler for Food

When you start looking to buy a long-term "food storage" cooler—as opposed to a drink cooler or one to keep food cold for an hour on the way home from the store—you'll quickly see that there is a huge price difference in various brands.

Do you really need to spend $300 (or more!) for a cooler?

A great deal of the decision depends on how rough conditions will be and whether you're thinking in terms of using it for months or for years.

Once you get into the coolers that are marketed as five- or six-day coolers, the insulation seems to be fairly equal in all of them regardless of price—about 2″ thick. The difference between the ones that sell for $100 or under and those going for $300 or more seems to be in the overall construction quality and features.

- On the more expensive coolers, the lid has a sturdy latch; on cheaper ones, it does not—just a "tight fit." Without a latch, it can be a real problem if the cooler tips over or slides off a seat!
- More expensive coolers have much more rugged hinges—important if someone in the group isn't very gentle. With a cheaper one, carry duct tape and be prepared to improvise.
- Many of the less expensive coolers have "drink holders" molded in the top, which seems like a nice feature until you realize that there is almost no insulation where the cutout is. Fill the cup holder with foam peanuts and duct tape over the top.
- The more expensive coolers tend to have places designed for tie-downs that are beefed up accordingly. With the cheaper coolers, you'll have to run lines to the handles—and the handles haven't been designed to take this type of load and may break.
- Drain plugs are more rugged on more expensive units, and less likely to leak or pop open (I never had a problem with ours, but I've heard people complain).

For long term usage—more than a few months—or in rough conditions and/or with large groups, initially more expensive brands such as Yeti and Engel are likely to be cheaper in the long run and less aggravating in terms of breaking and repairing or replacing. In truly rough conditions, a locking lid will more than pay for itself.

Beyond the brand, a few more thoughts on selecting a cooler for food:

- All-white "marine" coolers do a better job of insulating if they are sitting in the sun—but if you're going to throw a blanket over the cooler for extra insulation, it doesn't matter what color the cooler is.
- Soft-sided coolers are great for taking to the store or for putting food in while you defrost the refrigerator, but totally insufficient for long-term storage. They just don't have the insulation.
- I've never seen a Styrofoam cooler that was up to the task—the lids don't fit tightly enough and the Styrofoam tends to break.
- The Coleman coolers that are "steel belted" and look like the ones available 30+ years ago just aren't the same. They are not nearly as bullet-proof as they used to be and the insulation is not as good as in Coleman's Xtreme series.
- Inexpensive 12-volt "coolers" have way too large a current draw to use in most situations (about 3.75 amps at 12 volts and they run constantly, no on and off cycling—90 amp-hours per 24-hour day, or more than what a 12-volt refrigerator would use), will only chill items a maximum of 40 degrees F below the ambient temperature, and you can't put ice in them (unless it's in a plastic bottle) to add to the cold.
- The point above does NOT apply to the Engel Portable Refrigerator/Freezers and portable refrigerators, which also run on 12 volts but are actually portable refrigerator/freezers. They are much more efficient but also far more expensive. There are also other brands of 12-volt refrigerators, such as Dometic and Whynter that are also good—they use a little more power than the Engels, but are also less expensive.

What Size Cooler to Store Food?

A 65- or 70-quart cooler is about the minimum size needed to have enough ice and space for food. The larger the cooler, the more efficient it will be—if you use at least half of that extra space for more ice. If it just holds more food and air with the same amount of ice, it will be less efficient.

Make sure to measure the space where you intend to put the cooler and figure out where you might secure it if necessary.

Putting It All Together

It's one thing to know how to store individual foods or what to substitute for them. Putting that all into a meal plan can be tough the first time or two as you figure out what does and doesn't work.

While I've gone without refrigeration or even a cooler for four months on two different occasions, it was only after a number of shorter trial runs where I refined my techniques and recipes. Initially, I tried things over long weekends—trips of three or four days—where I knew we wouldn't starve if I did something wrong. Success on shorter trips convinced us that we could make longer trips. One key thing is to take advantage of opportunities to buy fresh produce and, if you have a cooler, ice.

Sample Four-Day Meal Plan

To give you some ideas of meals and how I use the most perishable items first, here are our actual meals from a camping trip in 2012.

Breakfasts

Cold cereal with milk or soy milk, juice and coffee.

Other options:

- Oatmeal—add some dried fruit and nuts if desired
- Fried, boiled or scrambled eggs
- Pre-cooked bacon

- Toast or bagels (peanut butter or jam optional)
- Yogurt with dried fruit, nuts and/or granola

Lunches

Couscous Salad—couscous, onion, cucumber, green pepper, tomato, oil, vinegar, salt, pepper, and a touch of sugar; individual cups of applesauce.

Ham Salad Wraps—a can of ham, diced onion, a sliced tomato, and some mayonnaise, all wrapped in tortillas. Tortillas are a good alternative to bread for "sandwiches" as they don't get squashed and they're far less likely to mold. Oranges.

The Boat Galley Salad (see Appendix B, page 123)—can of green beans, some extra pasta from dinner the night before, small can of corn (drained), onion, tomato, dried fruit, marinated artichoke hearts (use the oil from the jar instead of adding oil), dash of sugar, and balsamic vinegar. If we're really hungry, I'll add a can of ham, broken into bite-sized bits.

Snack Lunch—A small jar of peanut butter and box of Wheat Thins, a bag of nuts, a bag of dried fruit, a bag of carrots (also good with the peanut butter), and a little bag of olives.

Snacks

- Clif bars or other granola/trail bars
- Packages of dried fruit and raisins
- Individual packages of olives
- Jerky
- Nuts

Dinners

Tacos and a Tossed Salad—use a can of roast beef and drain/rinse the gravy off, break up or shred the meat, and heat it up with spices or a packet of taco seasoning. Serve with tortillas, salsa, diced onion, green pepper, and sour cream made from non-refrigerated ingredients (note:

111

you won't need a full batch of sour cream, so reserve some for the tacos and use the rest with your favorite dip mix to make an appetizer). Tossed salad with lettuce, tomatoes, a small can of black olives, and my vinaigrette dressing (see Appendix B, page 117).

Chicken, Apricots, & Almond Couscous—a can of chicken breast, dried apricots, whole almonds, a little flour, honey, and cinnamon, plus the couscous. Drain the liquid from the canned chicken breast into a pan and mix in about 2 teaspoons (5 g) of flour, a dash of cinnamon and a generous spoonful of honey. Bring it all to a boil and add the apricots. Simmer for five minutes, then turn the burner off and add chicken and almonds, mixing very gently. Let sit 3 to 5 minutes to warm through. While this is cooking, make couscous according to package directions. Serve chicken mixture over couscous.

Optional extra: Pan-Roasted Veggies—use a tablespoon of oil and sauté a bunch of mixed vegetables with a dash of salt and pepper or Mrs. Dash. Our favorite veggies depend on what looks good at the market but will often include zucchini or summer squash, onion quarters, baby carrots, and mushrooms.

Special Treat: Chocolate-Oatmeal No-Bake Cookies (see Appendix B, page 159) using canola or vegetable oil in place of the butter and either powdered or boxed milk.

Pasta Supreme—Sauté a can of shrimp or ham, onion chunks, and a (drained) can of mushrooms (or fresh if you have them) with some garlic and Italian seasoning. Add a small jar of sun-dried tomatoes in olive oil and a small (drained) can of sliced black olives. At the same time, cook pasta. Toss it all together and serve.

Chili, Corn Bread and Coleslaw—Make the chili with one can each of (drained) roast beef, kidney beans, and diced tomatoes, plus some diced onions and green peppers and a variety of spices. Make corn bread from box mix, using fresh or powdered egg and boxed milk. Bake in oven or in skillet. Coleslaw, made from chopped cabbage, a can of pineapple tidbits, a handful of peanuts, and mayonnaise.

Final Thoughts

You've made it through the whole book! There's a lot of information and it can be tough to absorb it all so that the concepts are second nature. Don't worry—it'll come with time.

Keep this guide handy as you're preparing a meal plan and shopping list in order to see what will and won't last. Use the main dish idea list (see page 10) to spark your imagination. And don't worry if things don't turn out perfectly at first. You're trying something new.

Meals without refrigeration don't have to be drastically different than what you eat now. I picked one family favorite at a time and created a "no refrigeration" version of it.

Gain confidence with a few simple meals first, working up in complexity as you master the techniques.

Remember, home refrigeration has only been around for 100 years or so, and people have been eating far longer than that. If our great-grandparents could do it, we can!

One of my favorite sayings is "Life's more interesting when you say yes!" It's only by trying new things that we get to do things that are out of the ordinary. What will you get to experience by saying yes to having no refrigeration?

Thank You So Much!

Thank you for buying this book and more importantly, thank you for reading it. I'm honored by the trust you've placed in me. I hope this book gives you the information, skills and confidence to do something so different from what most of us are taught from childhood: store food without refrigeration. I hope it lets you realize some of your life-long dreams.

From sailors to campers, canoers, scout groups, preppers, adventurers, and those living off the grid, people have thousands of reasons for being without refrigeration anywhere from a few days to years. I'd love to hear more about your plans and whether this book gave you the information you needed. Please drop me a note (carolyn@theboatgalley.com) or leave a comment on The Boat Galley's Facebook page.

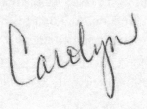

Appendix A

Instant-Read Thermometer Temps

Always remember to put the tip of the thermometer probe in the center of the food (not touching a pan or bone) and be sure to wash it thoroughly between foods to avoid cross-contamination.

Meats

Beef, Pork, Veal and Lamb . . . . 145° F*

Ground Beef, Pork, Veal, and Lamb. . . . . 160° F*

Steak, rare .120 – 125° F

Steak, medium . . . . .140 – 145° F

Steak, well done . . . . 160° F

Chicken and Turkey (ground, whole, or pieces). . . . . . 165° F*

Ham (fresh) . . . . 160° F*

Ham (pre-cooked) . . . . 140° F*

Sausage (raw) . . . . 160° F

Sausage (pre-cooked/brown & serve) . . . . 140° F

Fish

Tuna, Marlin, and Swordfish. . . . . 125° F

All other fish . . . . 135° F

Water

Water for yogurt . . . . .110 – 120° F

Water for yeast .105 – 115° F

Boiling water at sea level is . . . . 212° F

(to check thermometer for accuracy)

Baking

Quick Bread (made with baking powder or soda) . . 190 – 200° F

Yeast Bread .200 – 210° F

Cheesecake . . . . 150° F

Cake . . . . 210° F

Brownies (fudgy) . . . . 170° F

Brownies (cake-like) . . . . 180° F

Bread Pudding . . . . 160° F

Flan . . . . 175° F

Pie (pecan, shoofly, and other similar pies) . . . . 200° F

Pie (all others, including custard and fruit) . . . . 175° F

Miscellaneous

Egg Dishes (quiche, breakfast casseroles) . . . . 160° F *

Custard . . . . 160° F

Casseroles, Leftovers, and Stuffing/Dressing . . . . 165° F *

Baked Potato . . . . 210° F

*FDA Safe Cooking Temperature

Appendix B

Recipes

Basic Vinaigrette

This is a great basic dressing for just about anything. In addition to lettuce salads, it's good on coleslaw, pasta or rice salad, green bean salads or even tuna.

By varying the types of oil and vinegar used, you can change the taste considerably.

Ingredients (Per Serving)

> **½ tablespoon oil (olive oil, canola oil, vegetable oil, or flavored oil) per serving**
>
> **1–2 tablespoons vinegar (any type) per serving**
>
> **Salad**
>
> **Salt and sugar to taste**

Instructions

1. Put all salad ingredients in bowl large enough to toss the salad.

2. Pour oil over the salad.

3. Quickly toss the salad just to partially coat everything with oil.

4. Sprinkle salt and a little bit of sugar per serving over the top. Now drizzle vinegar over the top and toss again. Serve immediately.

A few notes

- You can vary the proportions based on your own preferences—this is far less "oily" than a true French vinaigrette—and lower calorie. A "true" French vinaigrette uses about 3 parts oil to 1 part vinegar.
- The amount of vinegar varies by whether the salad will "soak up" the dressing—pasta and rice will, but lettuce or tuna won't.
- You can add cheese or spices (basil, oregano, thyme are all good) for even more variations.
- Cider vinegar will give the sharpest taste, while the other vinegars are more mellow.

Greek Dressing

A true Greek Salad is a special provisioning-day treat
with fresh lettuce and other vegetables. But the dressing is
great on many other salads made with cabbage
or Napa cabbage as well as green bean and pasta salads.

A bit of an upscale vinaigrette, Greek dressing works well on any type of
salad and is also good as a dipping sauce for bread in place of butter.

Ingredients (Serves 6-8)

½ cup (125 ml) extra virgin olive oil or canola oil

¼ cup (60 ml) red wine vinegar

½ cup (60 ml) balsamic vinegar

3 tablespoons (45 ml) lemon juice or lime juice

3 tablespoons (16 g) dried oregano or Italian
seasoning

119

1 tablespoon (15 ml) minced garlic

1 teaspoon (1.5 g) dried basil or additional Italian seasoning

½ teaspoon (3 g) salt

2 teaspoons (8 g) sugar

½ teaspoon (1 g) ground pepper

Instructions

1. Mix all ingredients in a small bowl or bottle.

2. Toss with salad and serve

A few notes

- Best when made 15 or 20 minutes before use so that flavor can fully develop, but this should not sit unrefrigerated for more than an hour.

- Leftovers must be chilled. If serving less than 6-8 people, prepare in a smaller quantity.

Olive Garden Copycat Dressing

A really nice change from vinegar and oil dressings, yet totally no-refrigeration-friendly. Both Parmesan and Romano cheese are very hard cheeses and store extremely well at room temperature, but the dressing is good even if you only have one type of cheese or omit the cheese (which can also be done if someone is allergic to cheese). Good on all types of salads, not just lettuce.

Ingredients **(Serves 4-6)**

> ½ **cup (125 ml) mayonnaise**
>
> ⅓ **cup (75 ml) white vinegar**
>
> **1 teaspoon (5 ml) vegetable oil**
>
> **2 tablespoons (25 g) sugar**
>
> **2 tablespoons (10 g) grated Parmesan cheese**
>
> **2 tablespoons (10 g) grated Romano cheese**
>
> ¼ **teaspoon (0.5 g) garlic salt OR half garlic powder and half salt**

> ½ teaspoon (1 g) dried Italian seasoning
>
> ½ teaspoon (1 g) dried parsley flakes (optional)
>
> 1 tablespoon (15 ml) lemon juice

Instructions

1. Put mayonnaise in small bowl and drizzle the oil and vinegar in, mixing as you go so that the mayonnaise does not separate.

2. Add other ingredients and mix. Serve at once if the dressing cannot be kept cool;

A few notes

- Leftovers must be kept below 40° F (4° C) or discarded.

The Boat Galley Salad

I almost hate to call this a "recipe" as there are so many variations and substitutions available. You can use a combination of almost anything you have available and it'll be delicious!

Ingredients (Serves 4)

1 cup (250 ml) cooked brown rice

1 can green beans, drained

½ can corn, drained

½ can kidney beans, drained

2 tablespoons (25 g) chopped onion

1 medium tomato, diced

10 grapes, halved and seeded

2 tablespoons (1 g) sliced almonds

4 dried apricots, quartered

½ teaspoon (1 g) Mrs. Dash

1 teaspoon (4 g) sugar

1 tablespoon (15 ml) extra virgin olive oil

2 tablespoons (30 ml) balsamic vinegar

Instructions

1. Combine rice, vegetables, fruits and nuts in bowl. Sprinkle seasonings over the top, then drizzle with the oil and mix gently.

2. Add the vinegar and mix gently.

3. Serve immediately.

A few notes

- Leftovers must be kept below 40° F (4° C) or discarded.

- To make this into a more substantial meal, add a 6-ounce (150 g) can (the size of a tuna can) of ham or chicken. Drain the meat, and break it into bite sized pieces. Mix gently and briefly to avoid turning the meat into mush. Serves 2 as a main dish for dinner.

Subsitutions

Instead of this	Use that
Brown Rice	Any other type of cooked rice, pasta, couscous, diced potatoes, or barley, or cooked or uncooked crumbled ramen noodles (don't add flavor packet).
Green Beans or Kidney Beans	Garbanzo beans, black beans, lima beans, navy beans, peas, fresh or frozen spinach, or drained canned or marinated artichoke hearts.

Tomato	Cherry or grape tomatoes, canned diced tomatoes, diced peppers (sweet or hot depending on your taste), mushrooms, black olives, or diced avocado.
Grapes	Bite-sized pieces of fresh oranges, mangoes, papaya, apples, pineapple, strawberries, canned peaches, mandarin oranges, or pineapple.
Almonds	Cashews, walnuts, peacans, raw chopped carrots, jicama, broccoli, or cauliflower.
Dried Apricots	Almost any other dried fruit such as raisins, cranberries, dates, or bananas.
Mrs. Dash	Curry, cinnamon (use a little more sugar), chili powder-cumin mix, garlic, soy sauce, Italian seasoning, or tarragon. Note that these are all to taste as strengths of spices can vary greatly.
Balsamic Vinegar	Wine vinegar, cider vinegar, white vinegar, lemon or lime juice. Start with one tablespoon (15ml) and add more to taste.
Oil and Sugar	Of course, you can use a different type of oil or a sugar subsitute such as honey or a low-calorie sweetener.

Three Bean Salad

If I need a smaller batch for just two people, I make a variation with one can of green beans (no other beans or corn), half the onion, some chunks of fresh tomatoes, and half the amount of dressing.

Ingredients (Serves 4-8)

2 cans (15 ounce, 500g) cut green beans, drained

1 can (15 ounce, 500g) dark red kidney beans, rinsed and drained or black beans

1 can (15 ounce, 500g) cannellini beans, rinsed and drained or navy beans or garbanzo beans

1 small can (7 ounce, 250g) canned whole kernel corn, drained

½ small onion, diced

½ cup (125 ml) cider vinegar

½ cup (100g) sugar

⅜ cup (185 ml) canola or vegetable oil

> **1 teaspoon (5g) salt (optional)**
>
> **¼ teaspoon (1 g) ground black pepper**

Instructions

1. If possible, put the canned beans and corn in a colander for up to 30 minutes to completely drain them. Then transfer to a bowl with a tight-fitting lid and add the onion.

2. Mix all other ingredients in a small bowl, stirring until the sugar and salt are completely dissolved.

3. Pour the dressing over the bean mixture, place the lid on the container and shake to mix (stir the mixture if the lid is not completely tight). Let sit, shaking/stirring occasionally, for up to an hour before serving.

4. Serve with a slotted spoon to drain excess dressing.

A few notes

- Leftovers must be stored in a cooler.

- To make the Three Bean Salad more substantial add some chunked fresh tomatoes, cooked rice, or pasta just before serving.

- Add one additional can of beans for every two additional people (one can each for very large eaters). Vary the mix of bean types by what is available.

Healthier Zucchini, Carrot or Sweet Potato Bread

This recipe works well with either fresh vegetables or dehydrated. I prefer to use my dehydrated for this and save the fresh for other recipes where the difference is noticeable. If you don't have a conventional oven, it bakes well in an Omnia Stovetop Baking Oven—it will take about an hour but you'll need a double batch to fill it.

Ingredient (Makes One Small Loaf - 8" x 4" pan):

> **2 tablespoons (30 ml) canola or vegetable oil**
>
> **½ cup (125 ml) unsweetened applesauce OR a total of ½ cup (125 ml) oil, including oil above**
>
> **2 tablespoons (30 ml) water OR milk**
>
> **½ cup (200 g) sugar**

1 cup[1] grated zucchini, carrots and/or sweet potato (if using dehydrated, rehydrate according to package instructions to make 1 cup; diced is fine instead of grated)

1 cup (35 g) All-Bran, Bran Buds, bran flakes, raisin bran or Wheaties (if using flakes, crush somewhat before measuring)

2 eggs

½ cup (65 g) whole wheat flour (or white flour)

1 tablespoon (12 g) baking powder

1 teaspoon (5 g) salt

1 tablespoon (7 g) cinnamon

½ cup (75 g) raisins and/or walnuts (optional)

Instructions

1. Preheat the oven to 325° F (163° C).

2. Mix oil, applesauce, water, sugar, Splenda, zucchini, and All-Bran. Let sit for 10 minutes to let All-Bran soften. Mix in eggs. Add flour, baking powder, salt, cinnamon, and raisins. Mix until just combined.

3. Bake in a greased loaf pan at 325° F for 30 to 45 minutes. Bread is done when toothpick inserted in center comes out clean.

A few notes

- To fill a large loaf pan (9" x 5" - the size sold most often in the US), make $1^1/2$ times the recipe and bake for about one hour.

---

1   Metric weights will vary by the vegetable used. Instead of weighing, fill a 250 ml container. Exactness of measurement is not critical.

Yogurt

The basic recipe for yogurt is very easy—warm milk and a little yogurt from the last batch, kept in a warm place while the culture grows. As with many things, the devil is in the details, and attention to detail is crucial to successful yogurt-making. A good Thermos and thermometer are essential, as are the right ingredients.

Equipment and Ingredients

Thermos

You don't have to have a fancy yogurt maker, but you do need a Thermos to keep the mixture warm while the culture grows. The mix has to stay warm for 6 hours or longer, and so a really good Thermos is essential if you're in a cool climate:

- A vacuum-insulated Thermos is best; they hold heat better than foam insulation.
- A pint (2 cups/16 oz/500 ml) to quart (4 cups/32 oz/1 liter) size works well—pint is best for 2 or 3 people, particularly if you don't have refrigeration or a cooler.

Thermometer

A thermometer is essential. Guessing at the right temperature of the milk just doesn't work—a few degrees too hot and the culture will be killed; too cool and it won't grow. You need one that can read between 110° and 120° F—digital instant-read thermometers are easiest to read; analog ones don't require batteries.

Powdered Milk

Using powdered milk produces excellent results—use any whole milk variety (not the Carnation Non-Fat).

- Don't use a low-fat or non-fat milk. It is much harder to obtain satisfactory results.
- Do not use a brand with "added vegetable fat." These are widely available in Latin American countries, but the culture will not grow.
- The higher the fat content in the milk, the creamier the end result will be—and the more calorie-laden.

Yogurt Starter

You need yogurt with a live culture as starter. When buying commercial yogurt to use as starter, there are several points to remember:

- It must contain LIVE culture.
- It must NOT contain gelatin.
- The fewer additives, such as flavors, the better.

Yogurt drinks, particularly those promoted as digestion aids, can also work if they meet the requirements above.

In the US, you can buy special "yogurt starter cultures" in health food stores and online. These are great if you want to be able to periodically have yogurt and not keep it going all the time.

Water

The only real problem with water is that the stuff we put in the water tanks to kill bacteria (bleach, etc.) will also kill the yogurt culture. If your water has a chlorine smell or taste to it, let it sit uncovered for an hour or so to dissipate the chlorine before using it in yogurt.

Basic Yogurt Recipe

NOTE: The following recipe is for a 2-cup (half liter) Thermos. If your Thermos is larger or smaller, you will have to adjust the amounts accordingly, as the Thermos must be full to within 1" (2.5 cm) of the stopper for the contents to stay at an even temperature and the yogurt to culture well.

Instructions

1. Heat 2 cups (500 ml) of water to almost boiling (if it does boil, no problem). Pour it into the Thermos and put the stopper on. Let sit for a couple of minutes to pre-heat the Thermos while doing the next step.

2. Mix in small bowl until smooth: $3/4$ cup (95 g) powdered milk and $1/2$ cup (125 ml) water

3. Pour the hot water out of the Thermos and reserve in a container. Return about one-quarter of the hot water to the Thermos.

4. Add the milk mixture and mix. Check the temperature with your instant-read thermometer and use it after every addition of water. Alternately add hot water and regular-temperature water, mixing after each addition, so that Thermos is almost full (about an inch below where the stopper will come) and temperature is between 110° and 120° F (43° to 49° C).

5. If temperature is higher, let mixture sit until temperature has dropped into the correct range. If temperature is lower, remove some of the mixture and heat it, then return it to the Thermos and check temperature again. If temperature is too low or too high, the yogurt

will not culture.

6. Once the temperature is correct, add 1 to 2 tablespoons (15 to 30 ml) of starter yogurt or 2 to 4 tablespoons (30 to 60 ml) of yogurt drink and stir it in. The mix should come almost exactly to where the bottom of the stopper will come. Put the stopper back on the Thermos and put in a place where it can sit undisturbed for 4 to 5 hours.

7. After about 4 hours, remove the stopper and look inside. If yogurt does not appear thick, replace stopper quickly so as not to lose the heat and check again in 1 to 2 hours.

8. When the yogurt is thick, eat it or pour it into a storage container and keep it cool. If you leave it in the Thermos, it will continue to ferment, resulting in a very tart yogurt.

9. When eating the yogurt, be sure to reserve at least a tablespoon for use as starter in your next batch. If the yogurt took longer than 6 hours to culture, use 2 to 3 tablespoons (30 to 45 ml) as starter for your next batch unless you're trying to do a slow overnight culture (see tips below). I have found that the flavor and consistency of the first several batches gets better and better and it will culture more and more quickly until it gets down to 4 or 5 hours.

Tips & Notes:

- *The first batch can take considerably longer.* I usually find that when I start a new batch of yogurt from commercial yogurt or yogurt drink, it takes longer to culture the first few batches. I've had it take as long as 11 hours for the first batch! I think it's because many commercial products have a relatively low concentration of live yogurt cultures—even those that prominently advertise their health benefits.

- *If you want yogurt for breakfast and don't have refrigeration, start it before you go to bed and you'll have nice thick yogurt in the morning.* Save a tablespoon of the yogurt in a small container in the coolest place you can during the day, then make another batch at night. If it gets a little more tart than you'd like, use less starter so that

133

it takes longer to culture.

- *You will notice a watery liquid on top of the yogurt.* That is the whey. You can stir it into the yogurt or pour it off.
- *This recipe makes a very thick Greek-style yogurt.* If you prefer a thinner yogurt, decrease the amount of powdered milk by 2 tablespoons (5 g) at a time until it reaches the consistency you prefer.

Tasty Tuna Burgers

Excellent with lettuce, tomato, and mayonnaise.

Ingredients (Serves 4)

12 ounces (340 g) canned tuna, drained
2 eggs, beaten
½ carrot, grated
1/4 cup (40 g) Italian seasoned bread crumbs
1 green onion, finely sliced
dash of cayenne pepper
olive oil, canola oil, or vegetable oil
4 burger buns

Instructions

1. Mix everything together except the oil.
2. Shape into 4 patties.
3. Heat the oil in a skillet over medium-high heat. Place the patties in the skillet and cook for 5 minutes on each side, or until just lightly browned. Turn them gently as they can easily fall apart. (For this reason, it's hard to grill them unless you use a grilling mat.) Serve on a bun.

Tuna and Sweet Potato Patties

This can also be made with dehydrated sweet potato dices. Rehydrate one cup of dices with hot water, then drain and mash.

Ingredients (Serves 4)

1 medium sweet potato, peeled and diced

12 ounces (340 g) tuna, drained

2 eggs, beaten

2 tablespoons (20 g) bread crumbs

salt and pepper, to taste

1 tablespoon (15 ml) olive oil, canola oil, or vegetable oil

Instructions

1. Steam the sweet potato until very tender. Drain well, then put it in a large bowl and mash with a potato masher.
2. Add the remaining ingredients and stir until well combined.
3. Heat the oil in a skillet over medium-high heat. While the oil heats, shape the tuna mixture into 8 patties. Sauté the patties for 3 to 4 minutes on each side, or until golden brown. Serve two per person. We like a dab of Pickapeppa sauce on top.

Chicken or Beef Enchiladas
Ingredients (Serves 2)

> 1 cup (250 ml) canned black, pinto, or kidney beans, drained and rinsed
>
> 1 small onion, diced
>
> 1 can (8 ounces, 125 ml) corn (optional)
>
> ¼ cup (60 ml) sour cream OR ½ cup (125 ml) refried beans
>
> ½ cup (100g) shredded cheese—Monterey Jack, Colby or cheddar is best (may be omitted)
>
> ½ tablespoon (7 ml) chili powder
>
> 1 teaspoon (5 ml) ground cumin
>
> ½ teaspoon (2 ml) dried oregano
>
> salt and pepper, to taste
>
> 1 can (6 ounces/160g) chicken or roast beef, drained
>
> 4 small tortillas
>
> ½ cup (125 ml) salsa, diced fresh tomato, canned diced tomatoes, or tomato sauce

Instructions

1. Preheat oven to 350°F./180°C.
2. Mix the beans, onion, corn, sour cream, cheese, chili powder, cumin, oregano, salt, and pepper; stir to combine. Gently mix in the meat. Spoon 20% of the mixture onto each of the tortillas and roll them.
3. Place the enchiladas close together in a greased baking pan. Spoon the remaining mixture around and over the enchiladas and garnish with salsa on the top. Bake for 15 to 20 minutes, or until the cheese is melted and mixture bubbles.

Chicken or Shrimp Paella

Ingredients (Serves 2)

1 cup (250 ml) chopped onion or green onion

1 clove garlic, minced (or use garlic powder or garlic salt)

1 tablespoon (15ml) canola oil, olive oil, or vegetable oil

2 tablespoons (30 ml) chopped fresh parsley OR 1 teaspoon (5 ml) dried parsley flakes (optional)

2 bay leaves

1 small package saffron rice OR 2 servings any type of rice and 1/4 teaspoon (1 ml) saffron

2 teaspoon (10 ml) lemon juice, lime juice, or limón (Key lime) juice

½ cup (125 ml) dry white wine or broth (see below)

2 cups (500 ml) chicken or shrimp broth (use liquid from canned meat--see below--and canned vegetables, then make up the remainder with bouillon and water)

**1 to 1-½ cups (250 – 375 ml) chopped vegetables—
carrots, green bell pepper, broccoli, zucchini,
or mushrooms (fresh are best, but canned are
acceptable; see below)
1 can (6 ounces/160 g) chicken or shrimp, drained
and liquid reserved**

Instructions

1. In a pan with a lid, brown the onion and the garlic in the oil.
2. Add the parsley, bay leaves, and rice, stirring well to coat the rice with the oil.
3. Add the lemon juice, wine, broth, and veggies and stir well again. Cover and simmer until all the liquid is absorbed and the vegetables are tender.
4. Turn off the heat. Add the canned meat to the pan and mix gently. Cover and let sit for 2 to 3 minutes to heat through. Serve and enjoy!

Couscous Chicken

The ultimate in easy meals—great for a busy day!

Serves 2

> **1 cup (250 ml) water (use the liquid from the canned chicken and make up the rest with water)**
> **dash of salt**
> **⅔ cup (75 g) couscous**
> **1 can (16 ounces/500 g) diced tomatoes, not drained**
> **1 can (6 ounces/160 g) chicken, drained and liquid reserved**
> **½ teaspoon (2.5 ml) dried tarragon or dried oregano**
> **salt and pepper, to taste**

Instructions

1. Bring the water to a boil. Add a dash of salt and the couscous; stir well. Cover and turn off the heat—the couscous will cook itself in 5 minutes. Stir occasionally and check to see if more water is needed – the couscous should be tender to eat but not soupy (the correct texture is similar to cooked white rice).

2. At the same time, place the canned tomatoes in a small pan and heat them to boiling. Add the chicken, tarragon, salt, and pepper, and mix together as little as possible so as not to break up the chunks of chicken but enough that the ingredients are mixed. Place a lid on the pan and turn the heat off. Let the pan stand for 2 to 3 minutes to heat the chicken through.

3. Divide the couscous between two bowls and put the tomato mix on top.

Chicken and Apricots

Simple, easily stored ingredients that take absolutely no special handling. A real family favorite!

Ingredients (Serves 2)

> 1 cup (250 ml) water
> dash of salt
> ⅔ cup (75 g) couscous
> handful of dried apricots or white raisins
> 1 cup (250 ml) chicken broth (use reserved liquid from canned chicken; the remainder may be made from bouillon)
> 1 tablespoon (15 ml) oil
> 1 tablespoon (8 g) flour
> ½ cup (125 ml) diced onion OR 1 tablespoon (15 ml) onion powder
> ½ teaspoon (2.5 ml) ground cinnamon
> 1 tablespoon (15 ml) honey
> small handful of whole almonds

> 1 can (6 ounces/160 ml) chicken, drained and
> liquid reserved
> salt and pepper, to taste

Instructions

1. Bring the water to a boil. Add a dash of salt and the couscous; stir well. Cover and turn off the heat—the couscous will cook itself in 5 minutes. Stir occasionally and check to see if more water is needed – the couscous should be tender to eat but not soupy (the correct texture is similar to cooked white rice).

2. At the same time as the couscous is cooking, bring the apricots to a boil in the chicken broth and then set aside for them to plump up.

3. Mix the oil and the flour in a medium saucepan or skillet. Add the onion and cook until browned. Turn burner off and let pan cool 5 minutes.

4. Add the apricot mixture slowly to the onion mixture, stirring vigorously to avoid lumps from forming. When all of the apricot mix has been added, bring to a boil and add the cinnamon and honey. Cook, constantly stirring, until thickened to the consistency of gravy.

5. Add the almonds, chicken, salt, and pepper, stirring gently to keep the chicken intact. Cover and turn off the heat. Let stand 2 to 3 minutes, or until heated through. Serve over the couscous.

Roast Beef Chili
Ingredients (Serves 2)

> ½ cup (125 ml) diced onion OR 1 tablespoon (15 ml) onion powder or dried onion flakes
>
> ¼ green bell pepper, seeded and diced (optional)
>
> 1 tablespoon (15 ml) canola oil, vegetable oil, olive oil, butter, or margarine
>
> 1 can (10 ounces/300g) roast beef, including the gravy
>
> 1 can (16 ounces/500 g) kidney beans, drained and rinsed
>
> 1 can (16 ounces/500 g) diced tomatoes, drained, OR 2 fresh tomatoes, chopped
>
> 1 tablespoon (15 ml) chili powder, or more to taste
>
> ½ teaspoon (2.5 ml) ground cumin

Instructions

1. In a medium sauce pan, sauté the onion and bell pepper in the oil over medium heat until the onion is golden.
2. Add all the other ingredients, stir to mix, and simmer, stirring occasionally.
3. Serve immediately or simmer for up to an hour.

Pineapple Beef, Chicken, or Turkey

Ingredients (Serves 2)

1 cup (250 ml) stock of appropriate flavor (use reserved liquid, then add water and bouillon to make the full amount needed)

½ teaspoon (2.5 ml) garlic salt, garlic powder, OR 2 teaspoons (10 ml) minced fresh garlic

1 teaspoon (5 ml) paprika (optional)

½ cup (125 ml) fresh or canned pineapple chunks (juice reserved)

¼ cup (60 ml) wine vinegar or wine, divided

1 tablespoon (15 ml) soy sauce

3 tablespoons (40 g) brown sugar or white sugar

1 tablespoon (15 ml) cornstarch

½ cup (125 ml) water

½ cup (125 ml) sliced celery

½ cup (125 ml) diced green bell pepper

½ cup (125 ml) diced onion

2 tomatoes, cut into chunks (optional)

1 can (6 to 10 ounces/160 to 300 g) roast beef,

chicken, or turkey, drained and gravy/liquid
reserved

Instructions

1. Place the stock in a saucepan with the garlic salt, paprika, pineapple juice, and half the vinegar.

2. In a small bowl combine the rest of the vinegar, the soy sauce, sugar, cornstarch, and water; stir into a smooth paste and then set aside.

3. Bring the mixture in the saucepan to a low boil and add the celery and bell pepper. Cook 5 minutes. Add the onion and cook 5 minutes more.

4. Add the pineapple chunks and the soy sauce mixture to the pan and bring to a boil; cook until the sauce thickens, stirring constantly to avoid lumps from forming.

5. Turn off the heat and add the tomato and meat. Mix gently, taking care not to break apart the chunks of meat. Cover and let sit for 2 to 3 minutes to warm through. Best served over rice or couscous.

Goulash or Spanish Rice

If you use pasta, the dish becomes goulash; with rice, it's Spanish rice. Made with rice, it's good stuffed inside a green bell pepper and baked just until the pepper is tender.

Ingredients (Serves 2)

> **1 tablespoon (15 ml) canola oil or vegetable oil**
>
> **¼ cup (125 ml) diced onion or sliced green onion, tops included**
>
> **¼ green bell pepper, diced, OR 1 small can diced green chilies**
>
> **1 can (8 ounces/250 g) sliced mushrooms (optional)**
>
> **1 can (16 ounces/500 g) diced tomatoes, not drained, OR 2 fresh tomatoes, diced**
>
> **2 servings cooked rice or pasta**
>
> **½ teaspoon (2.5 ml) Italian seasoning**
>
> **1 can (10 ounces/300 g) roast beef, including gravy**

Instructions

1. In a skillet, sauté the onion, bell pepper, and mushrooms in the oil just until the onions are just light brown.
2. Add the tomatoes, rice or pasta, spices, and roast beef. Stir gently and cook until heated through. Mixture should be moist, but not watery. If too wet, simmer for a few minutes until just moist.

146

Jambalaya

Adding the optional beans and tomatoes makes this dish go further. If your spices are a little old, add more than what is called for. This dish should be spicy and flavorful but not uncomfortably hot.

Ingredients (Serves 2 without the optional beans and tomatoes, Serves 4 with them)

> ½ onion, diced
> ½ green bell pepper, diced
> 1 tablespoon (15 ml) minced garlic OR ½ teaspoon (2.5 ml) garlic powder
> 1 tablespoon (15 ml) butter, margarine, canola oil, or vegetable oil
> 3 to 5 green onions, chopped, including tops (optional)
> 1 can (8 ounces/250 g) mushrooms, drained and liquid reserved, OR 1 cup sliced fresh mushrooms
> 1 can (16 ounces/500 g) black, pinto, or kidney beans , drained and rinsed
> 1 can (16 ounces/500 g) diced tomatoes, not drained (optional)
> 2 servings brown or white rice, not cooked
> 1-½ cups (185 ml) stock (use the reserved liquid from the meat (below), then add water and chicken or shrimp bouillon to make the full amount needed)
> salt and pepper, to taste
> ⅛ teaspoon (0.5 ml) cayenne pepper
> ½ teaspoon (2.5 ml) chili powder
> 2 whole bay leaves
> ¼ (1.25 ml) teaspoon dried thyme
> ⅛ teaspoon (0.5 ml) ground cloves
> 1 can (6 ounces/160 g) ham, chicken, shrimp, or oysters, drained and liquid reserved

Instructions

1. Brown onion, bell pepper, and garlic in the butter over medium heat.
2. Add the green onion, mushrooms, beans, tomato, rice, stock, salt, ground pepper, cayenne, chili powder, bay leaves, thyme, and cloves.
3. Bring to a boil, then turn down the heat, cover, and simmer about 45 minutes or until the rice is cooked but still firm, stirring occasionally. If the rice is too liquid, remove the cover and turn up the heat to boil away some of the liquid. (All rice is different; you may have to add water.)
4. Add the meat; mix gently, cover, and let sit for 2 to 3 minutes to heat through. Serve in bowls.

Pasta with Ham in Butter Sauce

This is never quite the same twice. There are lots of options depending on what is available.

Ingredients (Serves 2)

2 servings of dry pasta (fettuccine, rotini, spaghetti, penne—almost any type will work)

1 beef bouillon cube OR 1 teaspoon (5 ml) salt

2 tablespoons (28 g) butter, margarine, olive oil, canola oil, or vegetable oil

2 cups (500 ml) total of any of the following:

- **green onions, sliced, including tops, OR diced onion,**
- **mushrooms, fresh or canned**
- **diced sweet bell or spicy chile peppers, any color**
- **sun-dried tomatoes, seeded and diced fresh tomatoes, or drained canned tomatoes**
- **artichoke hearts (in brine or marinated),**
- **small quantities of canned corn or peas**

1 tablespoon (15 ml) minced garlic OR 1 teaspoon (5 ml) garlic powder

1 can (6 ounces/160 g) ham, drained and broken into chunks

Instructions

1. Cook the pasta according to package directions.
2. At the same time, melt the butter in a skillet and sauté the mixed vegetables. When just golden, add the garlic and ham, mix gently, and heat through.
3. Drain the pasta and add to the pan, tossing to mix. Serve in bowls.
4. Variations: This is also good with cooked bacon or 1 can (6 ounces/160 g) chicken (use chicken broth to cook the pasta).

Appendix B

Rice or Pasta Salad with Ham
Ingredients (Serves 2)

> 2 servings rice or bite-size pasta (penne, rotini, bow ties, macaroni, etc.)
> 2 tablespoons (30 ml) minced onion
> 1 tomato, cut into 16 pieces, OR ¼ cup (60 ml) sun-dried tomatoes in olive oil
> ¼ green bell pepper, diced
> 5 black olives, cut in half
> 1 can (6 ounces/160 g) ham, drained and broken into bite-size bits
> 1 tablespoon (15 ml) olive oil, canola oil, or vegetable oil
> 2 tablespoons (30 ml) balsamic vinegar, red wine vinegar, c ider vinegar, or other vinegar
> 1 teaspoon (5 ml) sugar

Instructions
1. Cook the rice or pasta while chopping and prepping the other ingredients, drain.
2. Place the onion, tomato, bell pepper, olives, and ham in a bowl. Add the cooked rice or pasta and mix gently.
3. Sprinkle with the oil, vinegar, and sugar and mix gently. Serve warm (good on a cold day) or let cool.

A few notes
• For more variety, try adding one of these ingredients!
> Add 1 tablespoon (15 ml) pine nuts.
> Add cucumber—cut several slices 1/4 inch thick, then cut each slice into quarters.
> Or, Use canned chicken instead of ham.

Crab, Meat, Seafood, or Fish Cakes

This is a great "base" recipe that you can use with whatever ingredients you have on hand.

Ingredients (Serves 2)

Choose One "Binder" (or mix two):

1 medium potato, peeled, boiled, and smashed
2 slices bread, crumbled
½ cup (55 g) flour
½ cup (50 g) dry bread crumbs

Choose One "Moistener":

1 egg (the best moistener)
2 tablespoons (30 ml) mayonnaise or Miracle Whip
2 tablespoons (30 ml) milk
2 tablespoons (30 ml) reserved liquid from canned meat

Any or all of the following vegetables (Do not exceed 6 ounces):

¼ cup (60 ml) chopped onion or green onion (including the tops)

¼ cup (60 ml) chopped green bell pepper
chopped hot chile peppers, to taste
¼ cup (60 ml) canned corn
1 can (4 ounces/125 g) whole or chopped mushrooms OR ½ cup (125 ml) chopped fresh
mushrooms

Any or all of the following spices:
1 teaspoon (5 ml) onion powder or onion salt (if
no fresh onion or green onion was added)
salt and pepper or Mrs. Dash, to taste

Any or all spices for fish or seafood:
2 teaspoons (10 ml) Old Bay Seasoning
few drops hot sauce
2 teaspoons (10 ml) ketchup and dab horseradish, to taste
1 tablespoon (15 ml) salsa

Any or all spices for ham:
2 teaspoons (10 ml) prepared mustard and a
dash of ground cloves

Spices for corned beef:
1 tablespoon (15 ml) ketchup
1 can meat (6 ounces/160 g), drained
flour, for dusting patties
2 tablespoons (30 ml) oil, for cooking

Instructions

1. Mix the chosen ingredients in a bowl, adding the meat last so it will stay in large pieces. The mixture should be firm enough to form into patties but still slightly moist. If not, add flour or liquid to achieve the right consistency.

2. Form the mixture into two or four patties about 1 inch thick. Dust both sides of each patty with the flour.

3. Put the oil into a skillet and heat until a few drops of water sizzle. If the skillet is not hot enough, the cakes will be greasy instead of having a nice crust.

4. Add the patties and cook for 5 to 7 minutes, or until browned and crusty on the bottom. Carefully turn them over and reduce the heat. Cook for 7 to 10 minutes, or until browned and crusty and cooked through.
5. Serve hot either plain or with hot sauce (for fish and seafood), cocktail sauce, or mustard or pineapple sauce (for ham).

New England Clam Chowder

Ingredients (Serves 6)

¼ cup (60 ml) vegetable oil

1 onion, diced

2 stalks celery, diced OR ¼ teaspoon (1 ml) celery salt

2 cloves garlic, minced

2 bay leaves

⅛ (0.5 ml) teaspoon dried thyme

3 cups (750 ml) shrimp or chicken broth (may be made from bouillon) or stock

4 medium potatoes, peeled and cut into 1-inch chunks

1 can (16 ounces/500 g) corn, drained

36 ounces (1 kg) canned clams,* drained, juice reserved

2 cups (500 ml) media crema, evaporated milk, or milk

salt and pepper, to taste

Instructions:
1. Place the oil in a large pot. Add the onion, celery, and garlic and sauté over medium-high heat until the onion is tender.
2. Add the bay leaves, thyme, broth, potato, corn, and reserved clam juice. Continue to cook over medium heat until the potato is just tender—don't overcook or the potato will be mushy.
3. Turn the heat to low, add the clams and cream and mix gently. Add salt and pepper to taste. Heat just until warmed through—if you cook it too long, the clams will get tough (and the potato will get mushy). Remove the bay leaves and serve hot.

*If you don't have enough clams, use fewer, or mix in some canned chicken or ham.

Linguine and Clam Sauce

This is also good with canned ham, chicken, shrimp or fresh clams in place of the canned clams.

Ingredients (Serves 2)

> **2 servings pasta: linguine or other pasta such as spaghetti, fettuccine, penne, or rotini**
>
> **2 tablespoons (30 ml) olive oil, butter, margarine, canola oil, or vegetable oil**
>
> **¼ teaspoon (1 ml) red pepper flakes**
>
> **2 cloves garlic, minced, OR ½ teaspoon (2.5 ml) garlic powder**
>
> **1 green onion, including top, finely sliced**
>
> **1 teaspoon (5 ml) dried oregano**
>
> **1 or 2 cans (12 ounces/350 g each) clams, not drained**
>
> **½ cup (125 ml) white wine, milk, or water**
>
> **¼ cup (60 ml) cream, half-and-half (media crema), or evaporated milk**
>
> **⅓ cup (30 g) Parmesan or Romano cheese or other hard cheese (optional)**

Instructions

1. Cook the linguine as directed on the package while preparing the sauce. Drain.
2. Heat the oil in a skillet over medium heat. Add the pepper flakes, garlic, and green onion. Sauté just until the onion is soft. Add the oregano, the juice from the clams, and the wine. Cook, stirring occasionally, until about half the liquid is gone.
3. Turn the heat to the lowest it will go—the clams will get tough if cooked very long or at high heat. Mix in the clams and cream. Cook 2 to 3 minutes, or until heated through.
4. Serve by putting the pasta in bowls and covering it with the sauce, or by tossing the pasta and sauce in the pan and then serving it in bowls. Sprinkle with the Parmesan.

Ricotta Cheese

Homemade ricotta is quite easy to make. The biggest thing is that it needs to sit undisturbed for a half hour or more, and thus cannot be made underway. You'll need a thermometer and cheese cloth or other lightweight cloth (bandannas and old t-shirts work well). In total, the recipe will take about one hour to complete, but expect the first time you do it to take longer.

Ingredients (Yields almost 2 cups or a half liter)

> 6 cups water (1½ liters)[2]
>
> 3 cups (380 g) powdered milk
>
> 1 to 1½ cups (250 to 375 ml) white vinegar
>
> ½ teaspoon (2½ g) salt

Instructions

1. Mix the water and powdered milk in a large pan. Heat the milk over

---

2   This can also be made with 6 cups (1.5 liters) fresh milk instead of powdered milk and water. However, it won't work with boxed milk, which is ultra-pasteurized—it just won't curdle!

low heat to 120° F (50° C), stirring often so that the milk does not scorch.

2. When the milk reaches 120° F (50° C), mix in 1 cup (250 ml) of the vinegar and turn the heat off. Allow the mixture to sit undisturbed for 10 minutes—don't stir it, as the cheese will be developing curds.

3. After 10 minutes, you should see a lump of cheese in the center of a pool. If the liquid is clear, proceed to the next step. If the liquid is still cloudy, add a couple more tablespoons (30 ml) of vinegar and stir around the outside of the lump—you'll see more curds form. Continue doing this until the liquid is clear and no additional curds are forming.

4. Line a colander or strainer with cheese cloth or other clean cloth. Pour the curds and their liquid (it's the whey) into the colander. Pour a little additional water over the curds to rinse them, then gather up the cheese cloth and squeeze to get rid of as much moisture as possible. Continue to squeeze for two to three minutes to thoroughly dry the curds.

5. When dry, transfer the curds to a bowl or plastic storage container. Add the salt and mix.

A few notes

*   This can be used as ricotta in any recipe, and can also substitute for cream cheese in many dishes.

*   Any ricotta not eaten immediately must be kept chilled, so if you do not have a cooler you may want to make a smaller batch.

Chocolate-Oatmeal No Bake Cookies

Quick, easy and no baking! Great any time you don't feel like heating up the oven. In total, the recipe will take ten minutes.

Ingredients (Yields one dozen cookies)

> **1 cup (225 g) sugar**
>
> **¼ cup (62 ml) butter**
>
> **¼ cup (25 g) cocoa powder**
>
> **¼ cup (60 ml) milk**
>
> **2 tablespoons (40 g) peanut butter (creamy or crunchy; optional)**
>
> **1½ cups (135 g) oats (instant or quick cooking are best, but you can use Old Fashioned)**

Instructions

1. Mix all ingredients EXCEPT oats in saucepan. Bring to boil, stirring constantly. Boil 3 minutes (time it—too long and they'll get hard; too short and they won't become firm). Remove from fire and stir in

159

oatmeal.

2. For "cookies"—drop onto waxed paper or aluminum foil coated with cooking spray, oil or butter.

3. For "bars"—line a pan (I use a 7" frying pan) with aluminum foil and grease as above. Put mixture into the pan and press it down. Cut into bars when cool.

4. You can eat them as soon as they're cool enough to handle!

A few notes

*   Subsitutions can be made for many of the ingredients.

    Instead of butter, use margarine, canola oil, or vegetable oil.

    Instead of milk, use evaporated milk, prepared powdered milk, soy milk, or water.

    Instead of oats, use corn flakes, rice krispies, or a similar cereal.

John Herlig's Pickled Vegetables

This isn't a recipe for true pickles that can be stored for months, but rather for "quick pickles" that will last anywhere from a few days to a week without refrigeration. John uses it primarily to give a different flavor to canned vegetables and thus the combination of various vinegars and spices is important.

This will pickle about 1 cup of vegetables or beans, but every item is different in how it packs down in the container and thus how much pickling juice is needed. The items to be pickled must be fully submerged; if they tend to float, fill a plastic bag with water and use it to weigh the vegetables down in the pickling solution.

Ingredients

½ cup (125 ml) water

½ cup (125 ml) vinegar (almost any type—do not use malt or balsamic vinegar)

1 tablespoon (12 g) sugar

1½ teaspoon (8 g) un-iodized salt[3]

Spices to taste: white or black peppercorns, cardamom seeds, basil, oregano, rosemary,

3   Iodized salt can be used but the vegetable will have a reddish-brown color.

> thyme, dill, mustard seeds, hot pepper flakes
> or ground cayenne pepper, celery seed, garlic,
> coriander, marjoram, ginger, turmeric, smoked
> paprika, bay leaves or even curry powder/paste
> are good choices. Create your own combinations!

Instructions

1. Place drained vegetables in a small bowl or plastic container. Mix the above ingredients in a small saucepan until the sugar and salt are dissolved.

2. Pour pickling mixture over the vegetables and loosely cover. Let sit at least two hours for the vegetables to absorb the flavor; flavor will become more intense as time passes.

A few notes

- How long the pickles will be good without refrigeration depends on both the food and the temperature. In 80° F (26° C) temperatures, sweet or starchy foods such as corn, carrots, black, and pinto beans will only last a few days without refrigeration, green beans a week, and red onions several weeks.

Kimchi

Ingredients

1 medium head Napa cabbage[4]

¼ cup and 1 teaspoon un-iodized salt[5]

Water

1 tablespoon minced garlic

1 to 2 teaspoons grated ginger

1 tablespoon sugar[6]

1 tablespoon Korean fish sauce

1 to 5 tablespoons Korean red pepper flakes (if
you really like fiery food, you can use more based
on your taste)

Optional:

---

4   You can also use red or green cabbage or even other vegetables such as peeled cucumbers.
5   Using iodized salt will give your kimchi a reddish-brown color.
6   Do not use artificial sweeteners; the sugar is necessary for fermentation.

> **8 ounces (500 g) Korean radish, daikon or red radishes, peeled and cut into matchsticks**
>
> **4 green onions, trimmed and cut into 1-inch pieces**
>
> **2 carrots, cut into matchstick pieces**

Instructions

1. Remove core from cabbage and roughly chop into 1" (2.5 cm) pieces. Place in a non-reactive bowl or jar and mix $\frac{1}{4}$ cup of salt in. Add enough water to cover cabbage. The cabbage needs to stay down in the salt water for a day or so; weight it down with a plate or a plastic bag filled with water.

2. The next day, drain the salt water and rinse the cabbage a couple of times. Give it a final drain, but leave it damp. Place it back in the non-reactive container.

3. Add all the remaining ingredients and mix thoroughly, using (gloved) hands to sort of massage it all together. You need to work it until a pink liquid forms. Pack the vegetables down into the liquid and put the lid on loosely. Let sit.

A few notes

- The Kimchi can be eaten at any point—even on the first day—but will have the distinctive kimchi flavor as it ages.

- **Every day, mix the kimchi up and then pack it back down into the liquid.** Every day, give it a taste. This helps prevent mold. If you see or taste mold, it's time to pitch it.

- As the cabbage ferments, it will start losing its color and will begin to taste more like vinegar. It typically takes 3 to 5 days for this to happen but varies considerably with the temperature and size of the vegetables.

- Kimchi generally lasts at least one week without refrigeration and will last even longer in cool weather.

Appendix C

Equivalent Measurement Chart

When converting from US to metric measurements in the table below, I use "practical" measurements and not exact. For example, a quart is slightly smaller than a liter, but for practical purposes we can treat them as equal.

Many things that Americans measure in teaspoons, tablespoons or cups are measured by weight (grams) in the metric system. Since weight to volume is not a constant across all foods, there is no simple conversion table for that. The best way to convert that is actually to go by milliliters of volume.

Teaspoon	Tablespoon	Cup	Pint	Quart	Gallon	Fluid Ounces	Metric
$1/8$							$1/2$ ml
$1/4$							1 ml
$1/2$	$1/6$						2 ml
1	$1/3$						5 ml
3	1	$1/16$				$1/2$	15 ml
6	2	$1/8$				1	30 ml
12	4	$1/4$				2	60 ml
16	$5 1/3$	$1/3$				$2 2/3$	80 ml
	8	$1/2$	$1/4$			4	125 ml
	16	1	$1/2$	$1/4$		8	250 ml
		2	1	$1/2$		16	500 ml
		3	$1 1/2$	$3/4$		24	750 ml
		4	2	1	$1/4$	32	1 liter
		8	4	2	$1/2$	64	2 liters
		16	8	4	1	128	4 liters

About the Author: Carolyn Shearlock

Long ago, Carolyn realized that there were two essential ingredients for great trips: sleeping well and eating well. Food didn't have to be fancy, but it shouldn't be a gray blob, either.

Over the years, trips have progressed from weekend Girl Scout camping trips to more rugged adventures on three continents lasting as long as four months. Both through her own trial and error and advice from others, Carolyn has refined her techniques for storing foods and cooking tasty meals, sometimes with a tiny refrigerator, sometimes with a cooler and sometimes with no way to cool food.

From 2002 to 2008, Carolyn lived aboard Que Tal, a Tayana 37 sailboat and cruised full time with her husband. In 2010, she created her website, The Boat Galley, to help others navigate the challenges of provisioning, storing food and cooking aboard a small boat. In response to reader questions, the site has expanded to include buying a boat and gear, living on a boat, cruising and chartering, boat work, and potential problems.

In 2012, she and Jan Irons published The Boat Galley Cookbook, a collection of 800 everyday recipes and cooking tips they'd each collected while cruising with their husbands. It has become the go-to galley reference book for cruisers, and many RVers and campers also appreciate

167

the easy from-scratch recipes and extensive substitutions and variations to suit what's on hand.

In 2016 she began podcasting—find The Boat Galley podcast in your favorite podcast app. Carolyn, her husband Dave, and dog Paz now live aboard their second cruising sailboat, Barefoot Gal.

Food Index

A

Apricots, 32, 47

Artichokes, 32, 39

Asparagus, 33, 39

Avocados, 33, 49

Apples, 34, 48

Acorn squash, 34, 41

B

Bacon, 16, 18

Berries, 27, 32, 49, 62

Bananas, 32, 46

Bok Choy, 32, 42

Brussels sprouts, 33, 37

Broccoli, 33, 41

Beets, 33, 45

Butter, 76-82

   Brining, 79

   Butter Bell. 78, 79

   Canned, 77

Bouillon, 100

C

Corned Beef, 7, 12

Crab, 7, 12

Clams, 7, 14, 22

Chicken, 7, 11

Corn, 32

Chard, 34, 42

Cherries, 32, 49

Cauliflower, 33, 41

Cucumber, 33, 39

Cantaloupe, 33, 50

Carrots, 33, 38

Celery, 33, 38

Citrus, 34, 46

Cabbage, 33, 34, 37

Cheese, 83-86

   Powdered, 87–88

Cream, 71-75

   Media (Table), 71

   Coffee, 73

   Whipping, 73

   Sour, 74

   Powdered, 87-88

Condiments, 94-98

Coffee, 199

Canned Foods, 99

E

Eggplant, 33, 41

Eggs, 89-93

Powdered, 92-93

G

Green Beans, 32

Greens, 32, 41, 42, 54

Grapes, 32, 49

Grapefruit, 34 *See also* Citrus

Green Onions, 34, 36

H

Ham, 7, 10, 18, 115,

Hard Sausages, 18, 19

Honeydew, 33, 50

Hard Squashes, 34

Horseradish, 96

J

Jicama, 34, 46

Juice, 100

K

Kale, 32, 42

Kiwi, 32, 47

Kohlrabi, 32, 46

Kimchi, 54, 163

L

Lettuce, 32, 41

Limes, 34 *See also* Citrus

Lemon, 34 *See also* Citrus

Leeks, 34, 36

M

Mushrooms, 33, 42

Mangoes, 33, 47

Margarine, 76-82

Milk, 65-75

   Boxed, 66-67

   Evaporated, 67

   Powdered Regular, 68

   Powdered Buttermilk, 69

   Powdered Coconut, 69

   Powdered Soy, 70

Maple Syrup, 69

Mayonnaise, 96

Miracle Whip, 96

N

Napa Cabbage, 33, 37

O

Oysters, 14

Okra, 32, 43

Oranges, 34 *See also* Citrus

Onions, yellow, 34, 35

Onions, white, 34, 35

Onions, red, 34, 35

P

Pepperoni, 18

Peaches, 32, 47

Peas, 32, 43

Plums, 32, 47

Pears, 33, 48

Parsnips, 33, 45

Pomegranates, 33, 50

Peppers

sweet, 33
hot, 33, 39
red, 39
green, 39
yellow, 39
orange, 39
Pineapple, 33, 48
Potatoes, 34, 36
Papaya, 50

R
Roast Beef, 13
Rhubarb, 33, 38
Rutabega, 33, 46
Radishes, 34, 44

S
Salmon, 11
Shrimp, 12
Snow Peas, 32
Spinach, 32, 42
Summer Squash, 33, 41
Spaghetti Squash, 34, 41
Scallions, 34, 36
Sprouts, 56
Salad Dressing, 97
Stock, 100

T
Turkey, 11
Tuna, 11
Tomatillo, 32, 43
Turnips, 33, 45
Tomatoes, 34, 43
Tofu, 101

W
Watermelon, 33, 50
Wasabi, 96

Y
Yogurt, 70

Z
Zucchini, 33, 41

Index

Keep Learning
with Patoka Press

Take your favorite foods from the garden to the jar to the table with *Canning Full Circle*! Made to help both novice and experienced canners and preservers, this handy cookbook will keep your pantry - and stomachs! - full all year long. This unique canning coobook offers background canning knowledge, delicious recipes, and more!

Join Whiskey Professor Bernie Lubbers as he gives background knowledge on our native spirit. Included is a guide to traveling the Bourbon Trail, the history of Bourbon, delicious bourbon recipes, and more!

Patoka Press